Elementary Teacher's
September-June Book
of Classroom Activities:
An Almanac
for Every Day in the School Year

Elementary Teacher's September–June Book of Classroom Activities: An Almanac for Every Day in the School Year

June Dostal

Parker Publishing Company, Inc.　　　West Nyack, New York

©1977 by

Parker Publishing Company, Inc.
West Nyack, New York

Library of Congress Cataloging in Publication Data

Dostal, June,
    Elementary teacher's September-June book of class-
room activities.

    Bibliography: p.
    Includes index.
    1. Creative activities and seat work. 2. Schools
--Exercises and recreations. 3. Holidays--Hand-
books, manuals, etc. I. Title.
LB1537.D6   372.1'8'9   76-45394
ISBN 0-13-260810-3

Printed in the United States of America

HOW TO BENEFIT DAILY FROM THIS BOOK

- Do you have students who quickly finish everything you assign and then get into mischief because their minds and hands are idle?
- Have you wished for a collection of challenging, varied activities that you would be able to give to these students with the confident feeling that what you are giving them is not just mere "busy work" or is unrelated to curricular studies?
- Do you have students who habitually do not do well in most subjects and consequently have acquired a poor self-image, lack motivation, and have become behavior problems?
- Have you ever wished for a collection of fun-type activities to use as substitutes for the regular curriculum or as rewards for behavior modification?

If your answer to any of the above questions is "yes," then this book will be of real value to you.

Here is a collection of both activities related to important events as well as "fun-type" activities designed to stimulate creativity. This is a very practical resource for elementary school teachers and will enable you to select activities that involve an integration of various disciplines: language arts, social science, science, math, and others. All activities are centered around significant or interesting facts. They are presented in an almanac format, thus providing a continuous, day to day, flow of happenings and suggested activities relating to these happenings. Included in each chapter is a "Game of the Month" that can be played by students when they finish their almanac activities or at any time that the teacher feels such play would be desirable.

In classes where instruction is individualized, you can designate a portion of the classroom as the "Almanac Corner." Preferably, this corner will have available bulletin board space on which a large calendar of the current month may be posted. Such a calendar would be made up of 3 x 5 or 5 x 7 cards with one card for each day of the month. One side of the card would show the date, the reverse side would contain activities selected by the teacher from those outlined in this book which the teacher feels are appropriate for that particular class. Resource books should be readily available, either in the Almanac Corner, library, or in a Resource Center.

Students may be assigned specific times in the Almanac Corner when they can select at least one date on the current monthly calendar posted, turn over the card, and choose one or more of the suggested activities on the reverse side of the card. If desired, students may go to the Almanac Corner on a voluntary basis when they have finished all other assigned work.

To avoid duplication and to insure that all, or almost all of the dates will be selected, it is recommended that students write their name on a piece of paper and tack this paper to the date they have chosen. Thus, other students will know that this date has already been selected, and that they must choose another. This procedure could be followed for each month of the school year.

If the teacher feels that grading of the work completed in the Almanac Corner is essential, it is suggested that the grades be applied to whatever subject matter is related to the activity. For example, if the activity involved making a collage, the grade can be applied to art. If the activity was to conduct a science demonstration or experiment, the grade can be applied to science, etc. Also, if desired, the teacher may wish to weigh the various activities and assign point values or grade levels based on the degree of difficulty, amount of research involved, degree of creativity required, etc.

In traditional classrooms, the Almanac Corner can be utilized in much the same way as above except that the activities completed could be incorporated into the traditional subjects. For example, a student's report on the birthday of Alexander Graham Bell might become part of the science lesson; construction of kites to be flown in the March winds could become part of the art lesson, etc. Another alternative would be to select from the list of activities those that can be integrated into the existing curriculum and used as remedial instruction or for enrichment.

The Almanac Corner may be utilized each month or just for certain months, as the teacher wishes. To vary the routine, it is suggested that students sometimes be given an opportunity to choose the dates, and at other times draw dates from a hat, or have specific dates assigned. It is also suggested that students be permitted to trade dates with others if they wish.

The activities contained in this book are presented as a "springboard" for teachers. You will find it easy to utilize only those activities that are appropriate for the class' interest and ability level, physical surroundings, and availability of materials. For example, if you have a filmstrip, film, book, chart, tape, or other audio-visual that relates to a particular almanac activity, you may want to incorporate one of these in the suggested activities. Thus if you have a filmstrip on Alexander Bell, you may wish to add the activity of viewing the filmstrip and answering appropriate questions as one of the choices in the Almanac Calendar.

Additional dates can be added as they occur that are of religious, local, state, national, or international significance in order to keep the Almanac up to date. You might also wish to allow students the option of writing about or illustrating something significant that happened to them on a particular date rather than selecting from the activities listed.

Only the individual teacher knows the capabilities and limitations of students in a particular classroom. For this reason, I have included activities that will challenge and appeal to the exceptionally bright student as well as others aimed toward the slow learner-low motivation student. This approach will be helpful to readers who recognize the many advantages offered by individualized instruction.

June Dostal

ACKNOWLEDGMENTS

Appreciation is extended to Rudolph Dostal, Bob Buckley, and Tom Yackley for their ideas and assistance in completing this book.

The following games were adapted by permission of J. Weston Walch, Publisher, copyright holder: Beat the Clock Math, Vocabulary Maze, Multiplication Derby, History Rummy, Spelling Baseball, and Math Wheel.

Historical information and dates have been adapted from the book *When Did It Happen*. (Copyright 1957 by Stanford M. Mirkin. Published by Ives Washburn, Inc., a division of David McKay Co., Inc.,) Reprinted by permission of the publishers.

Table of Contents

Chapter One

September

1

"SANTE FE—ALL THE WAY" FIESTA

In 1692 the territory of New Mexico was taken from the Indians. The celebration of this event was started by the city of Santa Fe in 1712 and renewed in 1919. The fiesta usually continues for several days.

1. Investigate the early history of New Mexico and write a report based on your findings.
2. Using any medium you wish (crayons, chalk, water color, tempera, felt-tip marking pens, etc.) illustrate a battle which might have taken place during the conquest of New Mexico and the Indians.
3. Locate the state of New Mexico on a map. On a large sheet of paper trace or draw free-hand the outline of the state. Indicate on your map the cities of Santa Fe, Albuquerque, and other important cities. Also show important geographic features such as major lakes, rivers, mountains, deserts, etc. Your map should include the major industries of the state. For example, if a major industry is cattle raising, you might wish to draw or paste a small picture of cattle in that part of the state's outline where cattle raising is done.

PIKE EXPLORES PEAKS

In 1806 Captain Zebulon Pike and his exploration party accompanied by seven Indians started out to explore the West.

1. Investigate the life of this explorer and report on your findings.

2. Trace or free-hand draw a map of the U. S. Trace the routes Pike and his party traveled in their explorations.

FIRST WOMAN OPERATES TELEPHONE

In 1878 the first woman telephone operator, Emma Nutt, took her job as switchboard operator at the Telephone Dispatch Company in Boston. Up to this time telephone operators were men, but the company decided to employ women because the men were so rude to the customers.

1. It is easy to be rude on the telephone. Sometimes people are rude without realizing it or without meaning to be. Construct an etiquette book about telephone manners, or write a brief report on the topic, or make a large poster illustration using whatever medium you wish.

2. Recently many jobs which have been traditionally performed by men have been changed to include women. Talk to your parents and grandparents and other adults about this to see if they remember any such changes during their lifetimes. Investigate also the other side of the issue: jobs that have been traditionally held by women but are now changing because men are taking these jobs. Write a report based on your findings.

CHOP SUEY INVENTED

Chop Suey was first served by a chef working for a Chinese statesman, in 1896.

1. If the "cook" in your family makes this dish, ask for the recipe. Copy the recipe stating exact amounts of the ingredients and cooking time. Calculate the cost of all the ingredients used, energy used for cooking and its cost, the cook's time, and cost per serving. Try to collect other cooks' recipes for the same dish and do the same calculations for these. Summarize by stating which dish or recipe is the most economical in terms of cost per serving, energy cost, and cook's time.

2

WHO IS EUGENE FIELD?

In 1850 Eugene Field, a man who wrote poems and essays, was born. Mr. Field worked for several newspapers as an editor. At one time he conducted a column in a newspaper called "Sharps and Flats," in which he printed his poetry and short essays. Several of his poems have since been set to music.

1. Pretend you have your own newspaper column called "Sharps and Flats." Write one or more poems which you feel would be suitable for publication.

2. See if you can locate one or more of Mr. Field's poems or essays in your school or public library. Select one which is your favorite for reading to the class. Be prepared to explain the meaning of the poem or essay.

3. Mr. Field was, at one time in his life, an editor. Try to find out what an editor of a newspaper does. If possible, talk with an editor of a newspaper and ask him questions about his work: What does he do all day? What kind of training, experience, and education did he have? How much salary does a beginning editor usually earn? etc. Write a report on your findings.

4. Assume you are an editor of a paper. Write a short editorial about a subject of interest to you and your classmates. Remember that an editorial is not the same as news reporting. An editorial gives the writer's opinion or one side of an issue. Can you think of an issue and write your opinion or argument for one side or the other? Here are some sample issues to help you with your thinking, or perhaps you can think of others.
Recess (or lunch time) should be made longer (or shorter).
All students should be allowed to eat lunch at school (or at home).
Teachers should not keep students after school.
Teachers should (or should not) give homework.
Schools should not require all students to take certain subjects.
Schools should (or should not) be open all year round.

TREASURY ESTABLISHED

Congress established the U. S. Department of the Treasury in 1789.

1. Investigate the functions and departments of the Treasury. Write a report based on your findings.

SHERMAN ATTACKS ATLANTA

General William Sherman in 1864 occupied Atlanta, Georgia before starting his famous "March to the Sea."

1. Investigate the life of General Sherman and his contribution to the Civil War. Write a report on your findings. Include a map detailing his "March through Georgia."

3

SUMMER'S LAST FLING: LABOR DAY

Labor Day is an official national holiday. It may not always fall on September 3 because it is observed on the first Monday in September and the date changes from year to year.

1. Investigate the history of this holiday. Try to find out who first proposed a day in honor of workers, when it was first celebrated, and when Congress officially made it a national holiday. Write a report based on your findings.
2. Everyone celebrates Labor Day in his own way. How does your family celebrate this holiday? Write a short report (or illustrate in whatever medium you wish) explaining how your family usually spends the day.
3. Some communities have many activities planned for local citizens to help them celebrate this holiday such as parades, races, contests, concerts, ice cream socials, etc. What activities does your local community provide for celebrating? Write a short report explaining all activities available. Hint: You might wish to consult the newspapers, or call the city office or local park district office to determine exactly what is available.
4. Pretend you were given the job of planning your community's three-day Labor Day celebration. You must decide what activities will be done by the local citizens. Keep in mind during your planning that you must have a variety of activities for these three days which will suit all age groups in your community. Remember, too, that things boys like to do are not necessarily things that girls like to do. The same is true for mothers and fathers, grandfathers and grandmothers, etc. Also, try to have a balance between quiet activities (those that do not require a great deal of physical exertion) and strenuous activities (those that require physical activity). If your community has a Labor Day program of activities, you might wish to use this as a guide when planning

your own. Be careful not to merely copy it; be sure to make your own suggestions.

REVOLUTIONARY WAR OFFICIALLY ENDS

In 1783 the Revolutionary War between the United States and England ended with the signing of the Treaty of Paris. This treaty was signed by John Adams, Benjamin Franklin, and John Jay on behalf of the U. S.

    1. Select one or more of these famous Americans and report on their lives and contributions.

"SHENANDOAH" DESTROYED

In 1925 the U. S. Naval dirigible "Shenandoah" was torn to pieces while traveling over Ohio bound for St. Paul.

    1. Investigate to find out what a dirigible is, how it operates, what some of the famous ones were, and why dirigibles are no longer popular means of transportation. Write a report based on your findings.

    2. Using whatever medium you wish, illustrate either a dirigible in flight or the Shenandoah's mishap.

LOS ANGELES HAS A BIRTHDAY

The city of Los Angeles was founded in 1781 and celebrates its birthday every September 4.

    1. Investigate the early history of Los Angeles and write a report based on your findings.

    2. Using whatever medium you wish and a clean 9-inch or 6-inch paper plate, design a commemorative plate in honor of Los Angeles' birthday. Your design should have some reference to the city's historical background but you may also wish to include other things which represent the city of Los Angeles as it is known today—movie star homes, movie and television studios, orange groves, etc. You may wish to do some research about the city before beginning your illustration.

    3. Write a short paper explaining what the city of Los Angeles is like today. You may wish to consult current magazine or

newspaper articles for information. Be sure to include in your report the present population, major industries, climate, a map of California showing the city's location, and other information you think important.

4. The Los Angeles area was once known as the "Motion Picture Capital of the World" but this is no longer the case. Write a paper entitled "The Rise and Fall of the Motion Picture Capital." You will have to consult recent magazine articles for information. Try to find out how the film industry got started in Hollywood and who started it. Also try to find out why many of the major motion picture studios no longer exist.

HALF MOON SAIL

In 1609 Henry Hudson sailing in the ship, Half Moon, discovered the Island of Manhattan.

1. Write a report on the life and explorations of Henry Hudson.
2. Trace or free-hand draw a map to illustrate the explorations of this man.
3. Using whatever medium you wish, illustrate the landing of Hudson and his party on the island of Manhattan. You may wish to include Indians in your picture but be sure to consult a history book for authentic costuming.

MICE COATS INSTEAD OF MINK

In 1938 fashion experts predicted that coats made from the skin of mice would be fashionable in the winter of 1939. A full-length coat required 400 skins and cost $350. The cost could be lowered if people caught their own mice.

1. How do you feel about using the skins of animals for coats? Today there are many endangered species because their pelts have been used for making coats, shoes, handbags, etc. Research the topic of endangered species. Try to find out which animals are on the endangered list, and which are extinct because their pelts were valued for fashion's sake. Write a report based on your findings. Be sure to include in your paper your personal opinion about using animal skins for making clothes and for fashion's sake.

5

FIRST CONTINENTAL CONGRESS MEETS

In 1774 the delegates chosen and appointed by several colonies met in Philadelphia for the meeting of the First Continental Congress.
1. Consult a history book and read about the First Continental Congress. Write a report explaining its purpose, accomplishments, and which colonies were represented.
2. Using whatever medium you wish, draw an illustration of the meeting of the First Continental Congress. You may wish to consult pictures in history books to make your illustration as authentic as possible.
3. Assume you were a reporter present at the opening of the First Continental Congress. Write a brief news story about the event. Remember to include the five W's of news writing—who, what, where, when, and why.

BEEF SELLS FOR $48 A POUND

Steak which was shipped to Circle City, Alaska, sold for $48 a pound due to the Klondike Gold Rush in 1896.
1. Investigate and report on this gold rush. Include in your paper an explanation of why steak was so highly priced, and its price today.

6

THANKS, GENERAL LAFAYETTE

In 1757 General Lafayette, who assisted the United States during the Revolutionary War, was born in France.
1. Write a paper entitled, "Thanks, General Lafayette" stating the contributions this man made to this country's independence movement.
2. On the lighter side, how many limericks can you think up about Lafayette or the Revolutionary War? Remember the pattern for a limerick: five lines in which the first, second, and fifth lines rhyme, and the third and fourth lines rhyme.

Here are two examples to stimulate your thinking:

When General Lafayette first came to this land,
He landed with 11 companions on the sand,
And immediately this young man from France
Proceeded to make the British do a hot-foot dance,
As he pelted Cornwallis in a style that was grand.

There was a general called Washington by name,
Who was destined to be a man of great fame,
For through his efforts this country did win,
Its independence from England, which was no sin,
And the U. S. has never since been the same.

3. In a history book read about some of the famous battles of the Revolutionary War. Illustrate one or more of these using whatever medium you wish. Consult a history book to make your costumes authentic.

PILGRIMS SAIL

The pilgrims set sail from Plymouth, England on the Mayflower, bound for a new world, in 1620.
1. Investigate to find out why the Pilgrims left England, where they settled when reaching the New World, what settlements they established, what their customs and beliefs were, etc. Write a report based on your findings.

THE LAST OF THE MOHICANS

James Fenimore Cooper, an American novelist, was born on this day in 1789. While a boy he lived in a region where there were many Indians, and he learned much about them. He used this knowledge to write the series of novels about Indians and the frontier for which he is famous.
1. Read one of his most famous books, *The Last of the Mohicans* and write a book report on it. Use the book report style your teacher requests.
2. Learn what you can about the Indian tribes which once lived where you do now. Find out about their customs, rituals, beliefs, way of life. Write a report based on your findings.

3. Write a short frontier or Indian story. Try to make your story have a surprise ending. If you need help in getting started, try these opening lines:

> No one had seen any sign of Indians for the last three days but word was just received by messenger from Ft. Gilbert that Indians were on their way.

4. Investigate the life and contributions of this author. Write a report based on your findings.

HOOVER DAM STARTS OPERATION

In 1936 Boulder Dam, later called Hoover Dam, began operation.
1. Research to find out where this dam is located, what is the purpose of a dam, and what benefits are derived from it. Write a report based on your findings.

ST. AUGUSTINE SETTLED

The first permanent settlement of Europeans in North America was founded in what is now St. Augustine, Florida by a Spanish expedition headed by Don Pedro Menendez de Aviles, in 1565.
1. Investigate and report on the colonization of Florida.

"FOOL ALL OF THE PEOPLE SOME OF THE TIME"

In 1858 Abraham Lincoln made a speech in Clinton, Illinois containing these famous words: "You can fool all of the people some of the time; some of the people all of the time; but not all of the people all of the time."
1. Use this idea as a plot for a short story you compose. Try, if possible, to make your story have a surprise ending.

GALVESTON SMASHED

In 1900, 6,000 people died in Galveston, Texas when a tornado and a tidal wave destroyed the city.
1. Investigate and report on one or both of these phenomena.

WAR WITH JAPAN ENDS

In 1951 the war with Japan was officially terminated by the United Nations by the signing of a peace treaty.

1. Prepare a collage or drawing representing all the nations presently in the United Nations. You may use flags of the different countries, pictures of native costumes, or other symbols or ideas which represent the countries.

CALIFORNIA DAY CELEBRATION

In 1850 Congress passed a law admitting California into the Union.
1. Locate the state of California on a map. Using a large sheet of paper, draw free-hand the state's outline, or trace it if you wish. Indicate on this map the following: principal cities, capital city, major lakes, rivers, mountains, deserts, principal industries, and famous landmarks.
2. Pretend you had lived back in 1850 when California was admitted as a state and you were given the job of designing a state flag. You might wish to read about the state's early history before starting your design. You might also wish to consult the library to determine what California's state flag looks like today. Write a brief statement to accompany your design explaining why you choose the particular symbols, objects, or colors for your flag. Use any medium of your choice.
3. California had been a Mexican province before becoming a state. Many of its cities bear Spanish names. How many major California cities can you find that have Spanish names and what do each of these names mean? Write a paper based on your findings.

SEWING MACHINE INVENTED

Elias Howe received a patent for his invention, the sewing machine, in 1846.
1. Prepare a poster or bulletin board display entitled, "Look What You Can Do with a Sewing Machine." Include in your display actual samples or pictures of articles or fancy stitches done on a sewing machine.

HOORAY FOR PERSHING

General John J. Pershing, World War I leader, was welcomed home by one of the biggest parades ever conducted in New York City in 1919.

1. Investigate and report on the life and contributions of this military leader.

HOT DOG INVENTED

In 1927 an American meat packing firm announced the invention of the hot dog—a frankfurter with a zippered casing which should be removed after cooking.

1. Make a collection of your family's favorite hot dog dish recipes. Write each recipe in your best handwriting. Be sure to state all ingredients and give precise measurements. Include for each recipe the number of servings, price per serving, and source. Try to give each recipe in your collection a catchy name and if desired illustrate, using whatever medium you wish, one or more of your recipes to make them appear appealing.

BRANDYWINE BATTLES

In 1777 on the Brandywine Creek, Chadd's Ford, Pennsylvania, British General Howe successfully took Philadelphia, the then capital of the colonies.

1. Can you imagine what your life would be like if America had not won its independence from England? You would now be a British citizen and have adopted British ways and be educated in the British manner. Research British life to find how things in your life would change if you were now a British citizen. Some items you might investigate are the British school system, money system, government, weights and measures, speech, standard of living. Write a report based on your findings.
2. How creative are you? Can you compose the lyrics to a song about the Brandywine Battle to be sung to a familiar tune you already know? It might be a folk song or it could be funny or serious. Since most lyrics rhyme, you might begin by composing a short poem about the battle and then search for

a familiar tune that would fit your lyrics with minor modifications. Here is an example lyric to be sung to the tune of "On Top of Old Smoky." Perhaps you might like to continue the song.

> It was down near Brandywine
> That Gen'ral Howe got his fame
> He took Philadelphia
> And the col'nies were never the same.
>
> Now good Gen'ral Washington
> Fought the best that he could
> But Howe's men were superior
> And they done him no good.

Once you have composed your lyrics, produce a tape recording of your song, or lead your classmates in singing your song.
3. Using whatever medium you wish, illustrate the Battles of Brandywine. Try to make costumes as authentic as possible.

12

HUDSON FINDS RIVER

In 1609 Henry Hudson discovered the river that bears his name.
1. Write a report on the life and explorations of this man. Include with your report a traced or free-hand drawn map showing the Hudson River.
2. Using whatever medium you wish, illustrate this memorable moment in history. Try to make your picture as authentic as possible. You may wish to consult a history book to determine costumes of that period and to get descriptions or pictures of the Hudson ship.

DEFENDER'S DAY CELEBRATION

In 1814 the American forces successfully defended the city of Baltimore, Maryland against the British. Later this day became known as Defender's Day in Maryland and is a legal holiday.
1. Construct a time line showing major events in the War of 1812. Accompany your time line with a brief paragraph explaining each major event listed.

2. Pretend you were a newspaper reporter covering the Battle of Baltimore. Write a short news story on this event keeping in mind the five W's of news reporting.

HAPPY BIRTHDAY, WALTER REED

In 1851 Walter Reed, a famous doctor, was born.
1. Investigate the life and contributons of Dr. Reed.

AFRICA SIZZLES

The year 1922 marked the world's record for the highest recorded temperature of 136° F. at Azizia, Libya in Africa.
1. Investigate and report on temperature extremes as recorded by official weather bureau reports in different parts of the world. Find out which parts of the world have the highest and lowest temperatures and during which seasons.
2. Investigate and report on temperature extremes in the continental United States as recorded by official weather bureau reports. Illustrate your information in the form of a line or bar graph. Also include a geographic map of the U.S. indicating where temperature extremes have been reported.

"OH SAY, CAN YOU SEE"

In 1814 the words of our national anthem were written by a Baltimore lawyer, Francis Scott Key, while a prisoner on a British warship.
1. Write a brief history of our national anthem.
2. Some people believe that the words to our present national anthem are too difficult to remember. They would like to change our national anthem to some other song which is representative of the U. S. but has simpler words. Write a brief explanation stating whether you agree or disagree with changing our anthem. Be sure to state reasons for your opinion and give suggestions if you believe the anthem should be changed.

3. Using whatever medium you wish and keeping the words of our national anthem in mind, illustrate the scene Francis Scott Key must have seen which inspired him to write his poem.

15

HAPPY BIRTHDAY, WILLIAM TAFT

President William H. Taft was born in 1857.
1. Investigate and report on this President's life and contributions.
2. As President, Mr. Taft recommended the adoption of an amendment to the Constitution which would permit the levying of income taxes. Investigate to find out why it is necessary for this country to have income taxes, how this tax money is used, who supervises the collection of income taxes, how the tax is collected, and on what basis. Write a report of your findings.
3. During Taft's term there was a controversy over the conservation of natural resources resulting in resignations of officials. Write a report explaining what natural resources are and suggest ways that you and your family can personally help to save or conserve these resources.

HAPPY INDEPENDENCE DAY TO CENTRAL AMERICA

In 1821 the republics of Costa Rica, El Salvador, Guatemala, Honduras, and Nicaragua achieved their independence.
1. Investigate and report on one or more of these Central American countries. Include in your report the country's major cities, population, brief history, major industries, climate, and other points of interest.

16

CHEROKEE STRIP DAY

In some parts of Oklahoma, the anniversary of the opening of the Cherokee Strip is observed. This strip of land, in what is now the state of Oklahoma, was opened up on noon of September 16, 1893 to thousands of pioneers looking for new land for homes and farms. To make a claim a person had only to be the first one to arrive on a particular spot and plant a flag stake.

1. Pretend that you were one of the young men pioneers who decided to stake a claim to land on the Cherokee Strip. What things would you have to do after you staked your claim in order to live alone on the land? Explain in writing how you would get such essentials as food, water, shelter. What would you do if you became ill? What would you do for entertainment? Where would you get your clothing? How would you make a living?

2. Pretend that you were one of the young pioneer women who accompanied her family to the claim staked on the Cherokee Strip. Write a brief explanation of what life would be like as a young pioneer woman. How would you get food and water? What would you do if you or a member of your family became ill? Where would you get your clothing? Explain what some of the popular dishes would be that you would cook and bake for your family. How would you do your cooking, and what would your house probably look like; how would you do the laundry; what would you do for recreation, etc.?

DRAFT BECOMES LAW

In 1940 President Roosevelt signed into law the registration and drafting of men between ages of 21 and 35 for services in the armed forces. This law has since been discarded in favor of voluntary armed forces.

1. Write a short paper explaining whether you think the law President Roosevelt signed requiring young men to be drafted was a fair one. Do you think every young man should serve his country in this way? Do you think every young woman should also serve her country in this way? Why do you think this law was eventually discarded in favor of voluntary forces? Do you think we should go back to the draft system? Give reasons for your answers.

CONSTITUTION SIGNED

In 1787 the Constitution of the U. S. was signed.

1. When the Constitution was first ratified or approved by the required number of states, it was taken to New York, which

was the first capital of the government. Today our nation's capital is Washington, D.C. Write a paper explaining the different national capitals our country has had since the adoption of the constitution and the reasons for these changes.

2. Write a short history of important events beginning with the Declaration of American Independence in 1776 and ending with the signing of the Constitution in 1887. Include only major events which affected the final drafting of the Constitution.

3. Obtain a copy of the Constitution and read it, including all the amendments. Explain briefly in your own words the meaning of each article and amendment.

A DAY FOR ALL CITIZENS

By Presidential proclamation this day is Citizenship Day.

1. Either illustrate in picture form using whatever medium you wish or explain briefly in writing things Americans, including yourself, should do to be good citizens.

2. People may have different ideas regarding what a good citizen should be. Interview at least 20 people of different ages (a few younger than you, a few your age, and a few adults of different ages) to find out what they think are the characteristics or traits of a good citizen. Write a brief report summarizing your findings. State your own opinion about what you feel comprises a good citizen.

3. Pretend the mayor of your city appointed you as chairman of the Citizenship Day committee for your local community. What things might your community and school do to celebrate Citizenship Day? Explain in writing all the activities that would be used to celebrate this day.

18

CAPITAL GETS CORNERSTONE

In 1793 the cornerstone of the new capital building was laid by President Washington.

1. Many people visit Washington, D.C. every year. Assume that your class is planning such a visit this year. Prepare a list indicating points of interest which your class should see while visiting Washington and explain why you think each would be a good place to visit.

2. Collect pictures of famous monuments and points of interest presently located in Washington, D.C. which are related to our country's history. Prepare a large display of these pictures on poster board or the bulletin board and label each appropriately, stating its historical significance. You may wish to look through old travel magazines as a source of pictures or consult a travel agency for travel brochures.

3. Washington, D.C. has been our nation's capital for many years and will probably be the capital for many years to come. Pretend you were there when the site of Washington, D.C. was selected as the nation's capital. Prepare a brief argument for selecting a different city as the capital. Be sure to give reasons for your selection.

19

"I WISH I WERE IN DIXIE"

The famous Confederate war song, "Dixie" was first sung on this day in New York in 1859.

1. Write a brief explanation of the events which led to the creation of the Confederate Army and the beginning of the Civil War.

2. Besides "Dixie" there were other songs sung by both North and South which were popular and many are still sung today. Make a list of Civil War songs which were popular with the North, those popular with the South, and those still sung today. Also include the song writers' names.

3. Prepare a short tape of Civil War music of either one or both sides. Include portions or complete selections of popular songs. If you are an accomplished musician or vocalist, you may wish to perform some of the songs yourself.

M-I-C-K-E-Y M-O-U-S-E

In 1928 the popular cartoon character, Mickey Mouse, created by Walt Disney was first introduced to the public in a cartoon called "Steamboat Willie" in New York.

1. Investigate the life and contributions of Walt Disney and report your findings.

2. If you have an artistic talent and enjoy creating cartoon characters, perhaps you may be another Walt Disney. Why not try your wings by drawing a short cartoon strip based on

a cartoon character which was originally created by you and no one else?

3. Almost everyone has been entertained at one time or another by the many Disney cartoon characters in the form of comic books, stories, or films. Write a short paper explaining who your favorite Disney cartoon characters are and why.

4. Many people each year visit one of the two amusement centers created by Disney, Disneyland in California, or Disney World in Florida. If you have visited one or both of these, write a short paper or illustrate with self-drawn or cutout pictures what attractions you would recommend that a first-time visitor see at one or both of these parks. Assume the visitor has only one day for sightseeing and wants to see the best. How would you advise him and why? If you would like to visit, tell why.

STOCK MARKET PANIC

On this day in 1873 the New York Stock Exchange closed its doors for the first time. The trouble was caused by the failure of the new railroads to pay interest on their bonds which had been bought mostly by banks. People began to panic because they went to their banks demanding money and the banks could not pay. The banks had used their money to buy the railroad stock. The railroads had sold the bonds to the banks and promised to pay the banks a certain amount of money or interest but they never kept their promise.

1. Write a brief report explaining the difference between stocks and bonds, how the New York Stock Exchange operates, and its relationship to stocks and bonds.

2. During the Panic of 1873 many large banks closed their doors because they were unable to pay their customers the money they wanted. Today there are many safeguards to prevent this from happening. Suppose that you had deposited money in a bank which was now closed and you wanted this money. How would you feel? What would you do? Would this change your mind about putting money in a bank? Can you think of any ways in which a depositor's money might be protected? Write a paper explaining your thinking.

MAGELLAN SEARCHES FOR PASSAGE TO INDIA

In 1519 on this day Ferdinand Magellan, a Portuguese navigator, began his voyage in search of a western passage to the Indies.

1. Investigate and report on the life and contributions of this famous explorer.
2. Free-hand draw or trace a map showing all the voyages of Magellan and his company.

FIRST NEWSPAPER PUBLISHED

The *Pennsylvania Packet and Daily Advertiser*, the first daily newspaper to be published in the U. S., appeared on this day in 1784 in Philadelphia.

1. Skim through a complete issue of your local community daily paper to find out what features it has. Write a brief explanation of your findings. Explain the purpose of each feature. List those features which you feel should be left out because they are of no interest to you and suggest additional features you would like to see the newspaper carry.
2. A good news story has five essential W's—who, what, why, where, and when. Keep these in mind as you write a short news story about yourself, your classmates, or your school which you feel would be of interest to the people who read your community paper. If you wish, submit your story to the editor for possible publication.
3. Assume you have been asked to organize a classroom newspaper. Your must design the paper by deciding what feature departments your paper will contain, who in your class will take care of the news writing, producing the paper, financing, and distribution. Write a brief explanation of your solutions to these problems and state reasons for your choices of solution.
4. One of the ways newspapers make money is through selling space in the paper to advertisers for ads. The bigger the space, the bigger the ad, and the more money it costs. Look through some recent newspaper advertisements which particularly caught your eye. Write a paper explaining why you think you were attracted to each advertisement. Was it size,

color, position on the page, nearness to the front or back, size of print, drawings, picture, etc? Be sure to attach the ads that caught your attention.
5. Suppose you were going to advertise in your school or class paper. Using whatever medium you wish, prepare an advertisement. Remember the more colorful, the more imaginative, and the larger the print, the more likely it will catch someone's attention.

22

NATHAN HALE HANGED

Nathan Hale was hanged as a spy by the British on this day in 1776.
1. Investigate the life and contributions of Mr. Hale. Be sure to include in your report his famous last words.
2. Putting someone to death as punishment for a crime is considered capital punishment. How do you feel about capital punishment? Do you think it is right? Do you think the death penalty should be used only for certain crimes? If so, which ones? Do you believe the death penalty should be abolished completely? Write a paper explaining your views on this subject.

WITCHES HANGED

The last persons in the American colonies to be hanged for practicing witchcraft were put to death in 1692.
1. Investigate and report on the topic of witchcraft. Try to find out what it is, how and where it is practiced, and include a brief statement explaining your personal beliefs or disbeliefs on the subject.
2. Read a short story or novel which deals with witchcraft. Write a brief report summarizing your reading. Use the style of book report your teacher suggests.

23

LEWIS AND CLARK EXPEDITION

In 1806 the Lewis and Clark expedition arrived in St. Louis, Missouri after having successfully accomplished their mission.

1. Investigate and report on the life and contributions of one or both of these two explorers.
2. Free-hand draw or trace a map on which you indicate all routes covered by Lewis and Clark in their expeditions.

TIME CAPSULE BURIED

In 1938 on the grounds of the New York World's Fair, a time capsule was buried containing an assortment of objects representing present-day life. The capsule is to be opened in the year 6,929.

1. If you were on the committee which organized this time capsule, what objects would you want to be placed in the capsule? Write a report stating your preferences and reasons for selecting these particular items.
2. Use the idea of discovering a time capsule buried by an ancient civilization as the main plot for a short story you compose.

THE "BABE'S" LAST GAME

On this day in 1934 the famous baseball star, Babe Ruth, made his final appearance as a regular player with the New York Yankees.

1. Investigate the life and contributions of this famous baseball player and report on your findings.
2. Write a short paper explaining the present-day structure of the sport of baseball at the national level. Include in your report the names of all divisions and teams which comprise each division. Explain when and how the season usually starts and ends. Also include last year's standing of the teams.

PACIFIC OCEAN CITED

In 1513 Vasco Nunez De Balboa, a Spanish explorer, took possession of the Pacific Ocean in the name of Spain.

1. Investigate and report on the life and contributions of this explorer.

2. Trace or free-hand draw a map to indicate the routes covered by all of Balboa's explorations.

FIRST CONGRESS MEETS

In 1789 the first Congress of the U. S. met in New York. It adopted 12 amendments to the Constitution and submitted them to the states for ratification. The first ten were called the Bill of Rights and were accepted. The other two were rejected.
1. Read the Bill of Rights. Explain in your own words the meaning of each of these ten amendments. If possible, try to find out what the other two amendments that were rejected dealt with and why these were rejected.

YOSEMITE ESTABLISHED

In 1890 Yosemite National Park was established.
1. Yosemite is one of many national parks. Try to find out exactly how many national parks there are and where they are located. Trace or free-hand draw a map of the U. S. showing their names and locations.
2. If you have visited Yosemite National Park, either write a paper describing your experiences while there or present a slide or picture show to the class illustrating the beauty of this national park.

TWELFTH AMENDMENT GOES INTO EFFECT

In 1804 the 12th amendment providing for separate electoral ballots for president and vice president went into effect.
1. Investigate and report on the electoral system of electing the president. Explain in your paper how the 12th amendment changed the method of election.

EIGHT-HOUR WORK DAY ESTABLISHED

In 1926 the Ford Motor Company established an eight-hour work day, five-day week, for its employees. Prior to this time, employees worked much longer hours.
1. Today an eight-hour day, five-day week, is a commonly accepted fact of life. However, some companies are changing this by letting employees work less than the usual 40 hours per week or by allowing them to select the time of day or

night and the days of the week they wish to work. Some economists predict that in the future there may not be enough jobs for everyone to be employed and people will have to split their jobs with another person and only work two and a half days per week rather than the customary five days. By the time you enter the work force the customary eight-hour day, five-day week may have changed. Investigate to find out some of the new modifications of the traditional eight-hour day, five-day week and report on your findings.

FEDERAL TRADE COMMISION BORN

In 1914 the Federal Trade Commission was established. This commission was set up to maintain free, competitive business.
1. Write a brief report explaining the principal functions of the Federal Trade Commission and how it operates.
2. If you do not already know the definition of *competition* and *consumers*, find out. Then consider this statement: Consumers benefit from competition by receiving better products and services and lower prices. Do you agree or disagree? Write a statement explaining your opinion and include specific examples to support your ideas.

WOMEN ADMITTED AS DEMOCRATS

The Democratic Party admitted women into its membership for the first time on this day in 1919. This was done in anticipation of the ratification of the constitutional amendment permitting women to vote. The Republican Party soon followed suit.
1. Today there are many women actively involved in politics at the local, state, and federal level. Write a paper describing the political offices at the local, state or national level that are held by women. Include the title of the office and the name of the woman who holds it.
2. Today there are many active women's organizations. Investigate and report on the women's liberation movement.

List the names of these organizations, their organizers, supporters, purposes, and accomplishments to date. Mention in your paper any local women who belong to the movement with whom you are familiar and their accomplishments.

WOMAN ARRESTED FOR SMOKING

In 1904 a woman was arrested in New York for smoking a cigarette in the back of an automobile.

1. Arresting a woman for smoking may sound ridiculous now but at that period of time it was not socially acceptable for a woman to smoke. Those who did, had to do it out of the public view. Today the number of women who smoke is steadily increasing. Medical experts believe that the incidence of lung cancer and other disease is related to smoking. Investigate and report on the relationship between cancer and heart disease to smoking. Include in your report figures which prove or disprove women's susceptibility to these diseases due to smoking. Compare these to figures showing men's susceptibility.

TEMPERANCE LEADER BORN

Miss Frances E. Willard, a leader of the Women's Christian Temperance Union, was born on this day in 1839.

1. Investigate and report on the life and contributions of Miss Willard.
2. Temperance societies were formed to tell people about the evils of alcohol addiction and the advantages of abstinance (staying away from liquor). Today there are many people in our country, young and old, who drink alcohol. Some of them have become addicted to alcohol and may be classified as alcoholics. Make a study of alcoholism. Write a report of your findings. Include in your report the dangers of alcohol addiction and what happens to your body when you take in alcohol.
3. One of the organizations which helps those who have become addicted to alchol is A.A.—Alcoholics Anonymous. Investigate and report on this organization's function and how it works.

U. S. ARMY ESTABLISHED

A regular army was established by the U. S. War Department in 1789 when 700 men agreed to serve two years.
1. Investigate and report on the history and accomplishment of the U. S. Army.

NEW YORK WELCOMES DEWEY

In 1899 New York City extended its welcome to the hero of the Spanish American War, Admiral George Dewey.
1. Investigate and report on the life and contributions of this naval hero.

ARMY ECONOMIZES

In 1917 the U. S. Army publicized that it was able to feed 212 men 3 meals a day at a cost of $48.
1. Today American cooks are concerned with providing meals at low cost for their families. Survey at least 20 different families to determine how much they spend weekly on food, what general types of food they buy, and ideas they may have for stretching their food dollars. Summarize your findings in a written report. Be sure to include names of the participants in your survey.

ANESTHESIA HELPS TOOTH EXTRACTION

In 1846 Dr. William Morton extracted a tooth for the first time with the help of an anesthetic, ether.
1. Investigate the life and contributions of Dr. Morton and report on your findings.
2. If you are interested in dentistry as a possible career, investigate and report on this subject. Include in your report the education and training requirements, expected beginning salary, advantages and disadvantages of the job, fringe benefits, etc. If possible, interview one or more dentists for additional information about the career. Include also in your report specialities within the field of dentistry and requirements for these

3. Many people do not like to go to the dentist and will avoid it as long as possible. Of course, there are many things a person can do to prevent his dental check up from becoming a painful disaster. Using whatever medium you wish, make a poster display showing dental hygiene rules or tips.

September Game of the Month
Spelling Wheel

No. of players: 2, 3, or 4.
Grade level: Elementary
Materials Required: One gameboard (see diagram page 39); six decks of cards, each deck containing spelling words of increased difficulty taken from spelling books of different grades (100 cards to each deck), each deck numbered one, two, three, etc; one die; approximately 200 colored wooden, cardboard, or plastic chips (50 each of four different colors).

Rules:
1. Each player should select one of the four different colored sets of chips to be his markers. The six decks of cards should be shuffled and placed in their appropriate place on the gameboard. (See diagram of gameboard page 39).
2. Players decide by a convenient method who will go first. The first player throws the die. The number show on the die indicates the deck number from which that player's word will be selected. The player to the left of the player throwing the die selects the card from the appropriate deck and reads the word. The player throwing the die must spell within a reasonable length of time. The first spelling counts; there are no second chances.
3. If the player spelling the word is correct, he is permitted to place one of his chips in any of the segments within the concentric circle which corresponds to the number shown on the die thrown. For example, if the player threw a five and correctly spelled the word drawn from Deck Five that player could place his chip in any segment of the fifth concentric circle. If a player does not correctly

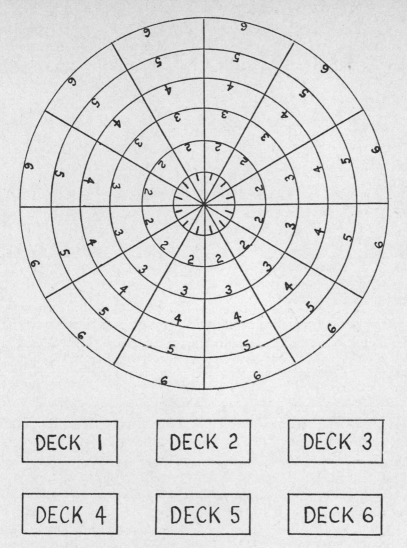

DECK 1   DECK 2   DECK 3

DECK 4   DECK 5   DECK 6

spell the word, he is not permitted to place any chips on the board during that turn.

4. Play continues in this way with each player taking his turn at throwing the die and the player to his left drawing the word card from the proper deck and reading the word.

5. Any player may displace another player's chips, if he so desires, when he correctly spells a word. Only one chip may be in any segment at any one time.

6. The winner is the first player who has chips in every segment of one of the concentric circles or has his chips forming a diameter through all concentric circles. See the diagram.

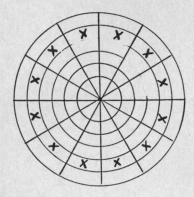 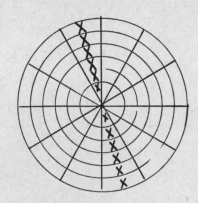

Variations:
1. The same game can be adapted to ages 7 to 12 by using first grade through 6th grade spelling words.
2. To extend the life of the game, players could be instructed to only use 50 of the 100 cards of each deck, or additional decks of cards could be made available containing other words, since it is assumed after several playings of the game players will eventually learn the spelling of the words within the decks.
3. The same game could be adapted to vocabulary words by using decks of increasing-difficulty vocabulary words to be defined. Each card could contain a word and give three or four choices of definitions. Players would have one chance to select the correct definition, or cards could just contain the word and players must supply the definition. In this case, the game might be called Vocabulary Wheel. Vocabulary words could be selected from several disciplines.

Chapter Two

October

1

"MARCH KING" CONDUCTS MARINE BAND

In 1880 John P. Sousa was made conductor of the U.S. Marine band. He composed many rousing marches and became known as the "March King."
1. If you have musical talent, perform one or more of Sousa's marches for your classmates either in a live performance or on tape.
2. Make a tape recording of Sousa's most famous music. You may include complete or partial selections of your choice. Your tape should also include some narration giving a brief history or background of each selection.

SPECIAL DELIVERY BORN

In 1885 special delivery mail service was first put into effect in the U.S. It was restricted to towns which had at least 4,000 population and involved an extra charge of 10 cents per letter for special handling.
1. If you are a stamp collector and have special delivery stamps within your collection, prepare a display of these stamps and write a brief explanation or history to accompany each stamp.
2. Pretend you have been assigned the task of designing a new special delivery commemorative stamp. Using any medium of your choice, submit several designs. Prepare a written ex-

planation to accompany each design describing its significance.

MODEL "T" INTRODUCED

In 1908 Henry Ford introduced his Model "T" Ford to the public.
1. Investigate and report on the life and contributions of Henry Ford.
2. The invention of the automobile had a great deal of impact on the American way of life. Think about what things you are accustomed to today that are dependent on automobile transportation. This may help you get your thinking started: Where would the roadside hamburger stand be today without the car? How about motels? And consolidated school districts? Can you think of more? Write a paper explaining your thoughts on the subject.

VEILED PROPHET SUPERVISES ST. LOUIS

Back in 1878 a group of St. Louis businessmen decided that a festival would help stimulate citizen pride in their city and attract visitors. They decided that the proceedings would be ruled over by a Veiled Prophet of Khorassan who would arrive by boat on the Mississippi River. His face would be concealed and his name kept secret.
1. Use your imagination and whatever medium you wish, and construct an illustration of what you think the Veiled Prophet of St. Louis might look like.
2. Today many cities and towns throughout the country sponsor festivals, pageants, etc., to stimulate interest in their town and attract visitors. Sometimes these festivals are related to a particular product or crop produced in the area such as cherries, pumpkins, corn, cheese, etc. Investigate your particular region or state to find out which towns or regions have some kind of celebration and what is being celebrated. Prepare a yearly calendar of such events in your region or state as well as a written report based on your findings.
3. If your local town or area conducts such a "festival" or celebration, construct several advertising posters, using any

medium, depicting the events of the festival. You may wish to distribute your posters in various places of business to help advertise the event. Obtain permission to do so first.

WHITE HOUSE CONVERTED TO HOSPITAL

In 1919 the White House was converted into a hospital after President Wilson suffered a stroke which caused his left side to be paralyzed.

1. Investigate and report on who ran the country when President Wilson was sick and explain the "chain of command" provided by the Constitution in case the president is unable to perform his presidential duties.

LINCOLN PROCLAIMS THANKSGIVING

In 1863 President Lincoln proclaimed the last Thursday in November as Thanksgiving Day.

1. If you had been president at that time, what day would you have picked to be our country's official Thanksgiving Day? Write a paper explaining your views on the subject and be sure to state reasons for your selection. Give alternate dates in case your original proposal is rejected.

"LOST BATTALION" HEROS

In 1918 Americans read of the heroism of the "Lost Battalion" in France. This unit was trapped by Germans at Binarville, France and believed to be lost. Eventually relief came and the men were rescued.

1. Investigate the history of World War I and construct a time line showing important events related to this war. Accompany your time line with a brief explanation of each event.

MERCURY CAPSULE ORBITS EARTH

In 1962 Navy Commander Walter Schirra, Jr. orbited the earth almost six times in a Mercury capsule and landed safely near Midway Island in the Pacific.

1. Investigate and report on the life and contributions of Mr. Schirra or another astronaut who has been in space.

4

HAPPY BIRTHDAY, PRESIDENT HAYES

In 1822 President Rutherford Hayes was born.
1. Investigate and report on the life and contributions of this president.

LINCOLN ATTACKS MISSOURI COMPROMISE

In1854 Abraham Lincoln made his first political speech at the State Fair in Springfield, Illinois. His speech attacked what Senator Stephen Douglas' speech of the day had said and asked for the Missouri Compromise to be repealed.
1. Research the history of the Missouri Compromise and write a report based on your findings. Indicate in your paper the effect this compromise had on the Civil War, if any.

COURT AGREES EDISON INVENTED LIGHT BULB

In 1892 the U.S. Circuit Court of Appeals upheld Thomas Edison's claim that he was the inventor of the incandescent lamp.
1. Investigate and report on the life and contributions of this famous inventor.
2. Thomas Edison is credited with many inventions. Find out what these are and illustrate in collage form on posterboard.

"SPUTNIK" STARTS SPACE RACE

The first man-made satellite, "Sputnik," which started the American-Russian space race was launched in Russia in 1957.
1. Investigate and report on the Russian-American Space Race starting with "Sputnik" up to the present time.
2. Some people believe that the U.S. has spent too much money in developing its space program while neglecting more important things such as medical research, poverty, education, etc. How do you feel about this? Do you think the millions of dollars spent for space programs were wasted? Write a paper explaining your opinion and stating reasons.

HAPPY BIRTHDAY, PRESIDENT ARTHUR

In 1830 President Chester Arthur was born.
1. Investigate the life and contributions of this president and report on your findings.

PIONEER IN TUBERCULOSIS TREATMENT BORN

Also on this day in 1848 a pioneer in the treatment of tuberculosis, Dr. Edward L. Trudeau, was born.
1. Research and report on the life and contributions of this doctor.

MEATLESS TUESDAYS AND EGGLESS THURSDAYS

In 1947 President Truman asked the nation to refrain voluntarily from eating meat on Tuesday and eggs and poultry on Thursday.
1. Pretend you were an American housewife during this period of time. Prepare a menu of one week's meals which will comply with the President's request. Your menu should include 3 meals each day, 7 days. It should contain all the essential nutrients from the four basic food groups as well as provide some variety. If you do not remember the four basic food groups, research this before beginning your menu planning. In addition, estimate the cost of each meal and cost per serving of the main dish for each dinner meal. Base your estimates on current prices.

GERMANTOWN ESTABLISHED

On this day in 1683 the first permanent German settlement in America was established at Germantown, Pennsylvania by 13 families.
1. Select an ethnic group of your origin or interest and investigate and report on their settlements and contributions to this country.

2. Using whatever medium you wish, illustrate your "family tree" tracing it as far back as you can. You may need to get the help of your parents, grandparents, and other relatives to make your "tree" as complete as possible.

TALKING PICTURES BORN

In 1927 the first spoken words in a full-length motion picture were heard thus giving birth to talking pictures.

1. Investigate and report on the history of the motion picture industry. Be sure to include the name of the first talking picture and its star. You might also wish to include names of some famous silent film stars, stars currently popular, and describe types of films currently popular. See if you can find out which films were the biggest money-makers in recent years.

"SEAWOLF" SUB SETS RECORD

An undersea record was established by the nuclear sub, Seawolf, when it submerged for 60 days.

1. Investigate and report on the history of the submarine.

PRESIDENT PROCLAIMS CHILD HEALTH DAY

By presidential proclamation every October 6 is known as Child Health Day.

1. You may not realize how fortunate you are to live in a country where most people are relatively healthy compared to people in other parts of the world. Americans have access to medical attention and facilities others living elsewhere do not. Of course, the way people live and take care of themselves has much to do with their health. Using any medium you wish, construct a poster illustration of ten rules for keeping healthy.

7

STAMP ACT CONGRESS CONVENES

In 1765 delegates from 9 colonies met in New York to attend the Stamp Act Congress.

1. Write a paper explaining the significance of this meeting and its relationship to the War for Independence.

NUCLEAR TEST BAN SIGNED

In 1963 a nuclear test ban between the U.S., Great Britain, and Russia was signed.

1. Since the signing of this ban, other countries have developed and tested nuclear bombs. Some people believe that because so many countries now have the knowledge to develop nuclear weapons, the world will destroy itself if there is another war. However, not all countries who have nuclear knowledge are willing to sign a ban on testing. Investigate the possible effects of a nuclear attack. Write a paper explaining why the world might destroy itself if it engaged in another world war.

RHODE ISLAND FOUNDER BORN

In 1637, John Clarke, one of the founders of Rhode Island, was born.

1. Investigate and report on the life and contributions of this man.

CHICAGO ON FIRE!

In 1871 the Chicago fire started.

1. Investigate the history of this famous fire which practically destroyed an entire city. See if you can find out the different accounts of the origin of the fire, why the fire spread so quickly, and how long it took to rebuild the city. Prepare a written report on your findings. If possible accompany your report with pictures or drawings.

FIRE PREVENTION WEEK

The week in October which includes October 9 is known as Fire Prevention Week.

1. Using any medium, construct a poster in honor of fire prevention week showing fire safety in the home or school or both.
2. Investigate the main causes of fires in homes. Compile a list of these and then check your own home to see if your house has any danger spots. If your find any dangerous places, be sure to notify your parents. Write a report explaining the results of your inspection.

NORSEMEN LAND IN NORTH AMERICA

This day is designated as Leif Erikson Day in honor of the landing of Norsemen on the coast of North America about 100 A.D.
1. Investigate and report on the life and contributions of this explorer.
2. Trace or free-hand draw a map illustrating the routes and explorations of Erikson and other Norsemen.

CALLIOPE PATENTED

On this day in 1855 Joshua Stoddard received a patent for the first calliope—a steam organ with an eight-note keyboard which he planned to sell to churches to use in bell towers for calling people to prayer.
1. Although the calliope was originally designed for churches, it was not accepted by them as the inventer intended. Instead, the calliope became popular as a source of music in circuses and on steamboats. If your have attended a circus or have ridden on a steamboat, write a paper describing your experiences, what you saw, what you liked and disliked, and how the calliope music sounded.

STAGECOACH MAIL ONLY TAKES 23 DAYS

On this day in 1858 it was noted that mail which traveled by stagecoach from San Francisco reached its destination in St. Louis in only 23 days, 4 hours.
1. Investigate and report on mail service in this country.

OKLAHOMA DAY CELEBRATION

The state of Oklahoma honors the founding of the first non-Indian settlement within the state by celebrating Oklahoma Day every October 10.
1. Investigate and report on the history of this state. Include in your report the first non-Indian settlement's name and by whom it was founded.
2. If you live in a state other than Oklahoma and your state does not celebrate a state historical day similar to Oklahoma's, pretend you have been given the task of organizing such a day. What special programs would you recommend be held at the state capital building in honor of your state's history? Explain the significant events in your state's history that you think should be observed during the celebration. What activities would you recommend to teachers and school children in honor of your state's historical day? Write a report stating your viewpoints.

U. S. NAVAL ACADEMY OPENS

In 1845 the U. S. Naval Academy opened at Ft. Severn, Annapolis, Maryland.
1. If you plan a military career and think you may wish to attend one of the U.S. military academies, investigate the academy of your choice and write a report explaining its founding, entrance qualifications, and location.

"TAILLESS" DRESSCOATS INTRODUCED

In 1886 the first "tailless" dresscoats for men were introduced from England. They were worn at the Tuxedo Club in New York. Although people were at first shocked by this kind of dress, eventually the "tuxedo" became more common than wearing a coat with "tails."
1. There have been many changes in fashion. Investigate some recent changes in either women's or men's fashions. Using whatever medium you wish, illustrate some of the fashions of

previous years. Be sure to indicate under each illustration the dates on which that particular style was fashionable. You may wish to consult your parents and grandparents for information about styles they remember. Also, consult old family photo albums to view the fashions.

A DAY FOR PULASKI

This day is designated Pulaski Day to commemorate the death of Count Casimir Pulaski, a Polish citizen who assisted in the Revolutionary War.

   1. Investigate and report on the life and contributions of this Revolutionary War hero.

FOUNDER OF Y.M.C.A. BORN

In 1821 Sir George Williams, founder of the Young Men's Christian Association, was born.

   1. Investigate and report on the life and contributions of this man.

EDISON INVENTS VOTE RECORDER

In 1868 Thomas Edison filed papers for his first invention, a machine which recorded electrically votes cast. He designed it to help Congress tabulate votes but Congress was not interested in it.

   1. Investigate and report on this invention.

COLUMBUS DISCOVERS AMERICA

In 1492 the famous explorer, Christopher Columbus first sighted the land of North America.

   1. Investigate and report on the life and contributions of this famous explorer.

   2. Free-hand draw or trace a map showing all the routes and discoveries of this famous explorer and his party.

3. If Columbus is credited with discovering America, why is our country not called Columbia? Investigate and report your answer.

A DAY FOR FARMERS

Also on this day in the State of Florida, some people celebrate Farmer's Day. The state legislature proposed this day to increase interest in agriculture.

1. Farmers are very important to our economy since they produce the food we eat. If you think you might like farming as a career, investigate and report on it. Be sure to include the qualifications, education, training required, average income for a beginning farmer, advantages, disadvantages, and fringe benefits.

U.S. NAVY ESTABLISHED

In 1775 the Continental Congress ordered the construction of a naval fleet, thus establishing the U.S. Navy.

1. If you are interested in the Navy or another branch of military service as a possible career, investigate the branch of the military which interests you to determine types of careers available, training, education, salary, benefits, advantages and disadvantages.
2. The first two ships constructed for the U.S. Navy were cruisers. Today the naval fleet contains other ships. Investigate and report on the different types of ships which now comprise the navy and the functions of each. If you have scale models or pictures of different ships, prepare a display to accompany your report.

PRESIDENT'S HOUSE GETS CORNERSTONE

In 1792 the cornerstone of the President's house, known as the White House, was laid.

1. Although the president's home is known as the White House because it is painted white, it was not until after 1818 that it

got this name. Investigate and report on the history of the president's mansion. Explain in your paper how the White House got its name.

14

HAPPY BIRTHDAY, PRESIDENT EISENHOWER

In 1890 President Dwight David Eisenhower was born.
1. Investigate and report on the life and contributions of this president.

HORSELESS CARRIAGE—A LUXURY FOR THE WEALTHY

On this day in 1899 the "Literary Digest" predicted that the horseless carriage, then a luxury for the wealthy, would never become as popular as the bicycle.
1. Write a paper entitled "Horseless Carriage Versus Bicycle." Explain in your paper what the horseless carriage was and who invented it. Compare the advantages and disadvantages of the horseless carriage and the bicycle.
2. Recently the bicycle has become very popular as a means of transportation. Many people are utilizing the bicycle not only for pleasure but as a means of transportation in order to save energy. Write a paper explaining whether you think the bicycle is a good means of transportation and a good way to save energy. State in your paper other ways in which you think energy can be conserved in the transportation process.

15

NATURE'S COLORFUL SHOW

In those parts of the U.S. which experience a change in seasons four times a year, this is about the time when Nature's colors are at her best as trees and shrubs change their leaf color from green to shades of red, orange, and gold.
1. Using whatever medium you wish, make a fall landscape entitled "Nature's Colors."
2. Make a collection of leaves from different trees. The leaves you select should be unbroken and pressed in a book for a

few days to eliminate curling. Identify each leaf and mount on heavy paper for display on the bulletin board.

3. Not all trees drop their leaves in the fall. Investigate to find out why some trees drop their leaves while others do not. Write a report explaining the process involved in changing the color of a tree's leaves and include the technical names for trees which drop their leaves and trees which do not.
4. What does fall and the changing of leaves mean to you? Write a paper entitled "Fall Is. . ."

HARPER'S FERRY RAIDED

In 1859 abolitionist John Brown staged a raid on Harper's Ferry, Virginia.

1. Investigate and report on the life and contributions of this abolitionist. Include in your report Brown's objective in his famous raid on Harper's Ferry.

APPLE TUESDAY?

Also on this day in 1904 several fruit growers decided to name the third Tuesday in October Apple Tuesday. They thought that setting one day apart to honor the apple would improve the sales of their crop.

1. The legend of Johnny Appleseed is a famous one. Investigate this legend and briefly report on your findings. Was there a real Johnny Appleseed? What did he do and why?
2. Apples were first called Peckers. Investigate and report on the history of the apple. Try to find out how many different varieties of apples exist today and where different varieties are grown.
3. Prepare a recipe booklet of apple recipes collected from relatives and friends in honor of Apple Tuesday. Copy each in your best handwriting giving exact measurements and directions for preparation. Indicate number of servings for each recipe and cost per serving. If you desire, illustrate some of the recipes using the medium of your choice. Be sure to give sources for each recipe in your collection.

17

CANAL OPENED

In 1829 a 14-mile long canal connecting the Delaware River and Chesapeake Bay was opened.

   1. At one point in our country's history, canals were a major means of transportation. Write a paper describing how canals were used for transportation and where the major ones were located. Include a map showing the location of the major canals.

STEEL-MAKING PROCESS PATENTED

In 1855 Englishman, Henry Bessemer, obtained a patent for his process for making steel.

   1. How is steel made and from what? Research this and write a paper describing your findings. Indicate in your paper the major steel-producing cities in our country.
   2. Investigate and report on the life and contributions of this famous steel manufacturer.

EINSTEIN ARRIVES IN U.S.

In 1933 Dr Albert Einstein, a refugee from Nazi Germany, arrived in the U.S. and made Princeton, New Jersey his home.

   1. Investigate and report on the life and contributions of this famous scientist.
   2. Why was it necessary for Dr. Einstein to flee Germany? What did he fear from the Nazis? Research these questions and report on your findings.

18

ALASKA TRANSFERRED FROM RUSSIAN OWNERSHIP

This day is the anniversary of the transfer of Alaska from Russia to the U.S. This occurred in 1867.

   1. Research the state of Alaska. Write a report on its history, industries, major cities, current population, and natural resources.
   2. Hand draw or trace a large map of Alaska. Show on your map its major cities, capital city, major rivers, mountains,

and location of natural resources. You may wish to use collage to show location of resources.

FIRST TELEGRAPH CABLE LAID

Also on this day in 1842 Samuel Morse laid the first telegraph cable in New York harbor.
   1. Investigate the life and contributions of this famous inventor. Write a report on your findings.

LONG-DISTANCE TELEPHONE LINE OPENED

In 1892 the first commercial long-distance telephone line was opened between New York and Chicago.
   1. Today long distance calling is taken for granted by many people and is much cheaper than when it was first introduced. Find out the price of a 3-minute call from your city to New York and Chicago. Also find out when rates are more expensive and when they are less expensive and why.
   1. Include in your report an explanation of why the price of long distance calls has generally decreased from what is many years ago. You may wish to contact the local telephone company for assistance.

U.S. FLAG RAISED IN PUERTO RICO

In 1898 the U.S. flag was raised over the island of Puerto Rico.
   1. Investigate and report on this U.S. territory. Include in your paper its history, major industries, major cities, capital city, and natural resources. If you wish, include with your report a map of the territory showing points of interest. You may wish to contact a local travel agency for information on the island.
   2. Free-hand draw or trace a large map of Puerto Rico. Prepare a collage indicating major cities, natural resources, and other points of interest you feel are important.

HAPPY BIRTHDAY, PRESIDENT ADAMS

On this day President John Adams was born in 1735.
   1. Investigate the life and contributions of this famous American and report on your findings.

REVOLUTIONARY WAR ENDS

In 1781 Lord Cornwallis surrendered at Yorktown, Virginia to American and French troops bringing an end to the Revolutionary War.

1. Assume you were a newspaper reporter present at this important moment in our history. Write a short news story about the event. Remember the five W's of news reporting.
2. Write a report on the major or significant battles of the Revolutionary War concluding with the surrender at Yorktown.

"GREATEST SHOW ON EARTH"

In 1873 P.T. Barnum opened his show, the Hippodrome, in New York City and called it the "Greatest Show on Earth."

1. Investigate and report on the life and contributions of this famous showman.
2. If you have been to a circus or carnival, write a paper called "Impressions of the Circus (or Carnival)." Describe in your paper the sights, smells, sounds, and tastes and feelings of a visitor attending the circus or carnival.
3. Read a short story or novel, either fiction or nonfiction, which deals with a circus or carnival. Report on your reading using the form your teacher suggests.

EDISON INVENTS LIGHT BULB

The first workable electric incandescent lamp was invented by Thomas Edison in 1879 after experimenting for 14 months.

1. Prepare a written or oral report explaining how the light bulb works. Include with your report a visual aid (drawing, picture, illustration on chalkboard, etc.).
2. Prepare a poster or bulletin board illustration entitled "Pointers to Remember when Using Lights " illustrating energy and vision conservation tips

22

THE "MET" OPENS

In 1833 the Metropolitan Opera House in New York celebrated its grand opening by performing Gounod's opera, Faust.
1. Listen to some opera music either on television, radio, or records or tapes. Make a short tape recording of your favorite selections from opera music. Include the entire selection or just partial selections, vocal or instrumental, or both, as you wish. Be sure to identify each opera selection by title and author.
2. Select a famous opera composer or vocal star. Investigate and report on the life and contributions of that person.

THOUSANDS FLU STRICKEN

On this day in 1918 it was reported that nearly ¼ of the people in the U.S. had been striken by influenza (flu). Up to this point in time between 400,000 and 500,000 had died.
1. Although we still have flu epidemics today, they have not been as severe as the one which swept the country in 1918. Perhaps one of the reasons for this is the invention of the flu vaccine. Investigate the topic of "vaccination" and report on your findings. Include in your paper the person who invented the process, how vaccines are produced, and the major diseases in this country which have been almost eliminated by the use of vaccines.

23

FIRST WOMAN FLIES AN AIRPLANE

In 1910 the first woman to make a public airplane flight by herself was Blanche S. Scott who rose to a height of 12 feet.
1. Although today rising to the height of 12 feet in an airplane does not seem very stupendous, it was considered an important feat in 1910. Have you done something by yourself which you considered an important accomplishment? If so, explain in poetry or prose form.

WOMEN INVADE NEW YORK CITY

In 1915 the City of New York was invaded by 25,000 women who marched down the streets demanding women's suffrage in all 48 states.

1. Investigate and report on leaders of the women's suffrage movement. Include in your report the point in history when women received the vote in all 48 states and how this was accomplished.
2. Another movement toward gaining equal rights for women is the Equal Rights Amendment to the Constitution, which at the time of this writing has not been passed by a sufficient number of states to make the amendment law. Investigate and report on the pro's and con's of this proposed amendment. Include in your paper your own position on the amendment and state reasons why you favor or oppose it.

MAINE DECLARED DISASTER AREA

The state of Maine was declared a disaster area after a large forest fire destroyed thousands of acres in 1947.

1. Using any medium you wish, prepare a posterboard or bulletin board illustration of outdoor fire prevention rules.
2. Investigate and report on the topic, "Aftermaths of a Forest Fire." Include in your paper the ecological effects of forest fires. If possible, include pictures or drawings showing the aftereffects of a forest fire.

UNITED NATIONS DAY

This day is United Nations Day in honor of the founding of this international organization designed to help maintain world peace and security, and to promote respect for human freedom.

1. Investigate the history and structure of the U.N. and report on your findings.

PENNSYLVANIA DAY

This day is also known as Pennsylvania Day in honor of the birth of William Penn, the founder of the state.

1. Investigate and report on the life and contributions of William Penn.

FIRST TELEGRAM SENT CROSS-COUNTRY

On this day in 1861 the first telegram was sent across the U.S. from California to Washington, D.C. and from San Francisco to New York.

1. Investigate the invention of the telegraph. Report on this topic and include in your report the significance of this invention and its use in modern-day life.
2. Construct a sample model of a telegraph. Consult a science book for assistance and briefly demonstrate your model for your teacher and/or classmates.

NYLONS GO ON SALE

In 1939 women's hosiery made of nylon, a synthetic fabric, was placed on sale for the first time.

1. Nylon is one of many synthetic fabrics offered for sale today. Investigate and report on the invention of nylon or other synthetic fabrics. State in your paper the uses to which each synthetic fabric is put.

SMOG CRIPPLES LOS ANGELES

In 1955 Los Angeles endured 18 days of smog (fog and smoke).

1. Environmentalists are becoming increasingly concerned about pollution of the air, water, etc., and its effects on our environment. Using whatever medium you wish, construct a poster showing several ways in which people can help protect their environment by reducing any form of pollution.

"TEAPOT DOME SCANDALS"

In 1923 the "Teapot Dome Scandal" started to unfold.

1. Investigate and report on this governmental scandal.
2. Recently our government has had another scandal called Watergate. Investigate this scandal and report on your findings. Are there any similarities between Watergate and Teapot Dome?

CABINET MEETING TELEVISED

In 1954 American people for the first time were able to view a session of the president's cabinet because it was televised.

1. Briefly report on the invention and purpose of the president's cabinet. Find out who comprises the president's cabinet today and what offices they hold.

26

ERIE CANAL OPENS

In 1825 the Erie Canal, which extended from Buffalo to Albany and connected Lake Erie with the Hudson River, opened to traffic. This was the first man-made waterway.

1. Investigate and report on the topic, "Canals—A Means of Transportation." Mention in your paper the major canals used in this country and how traffic traveled on these waterways.
2. Using any medium you wish, prepare an illustration of transportation on a canal.

COFFEE HOARDING BEGINS

On this day in 1949 Americans started hoarding (saving) coffee because a shortage of coffee caused by crop failures occurred.

1. Investigate and report on how and where coffee is grown. Explain what elements might cause a crop failure resulting in a shortage of coffee.
2. Economists refer to a law called "Supply and Demand." Investigate and report on what this law means and explain its effect on people and coffee back in 1949.
3. Prepare a large map either free-hand drawn or traced showing the principal coffee-growing areas of the world.

27

HAPPY BIRTHDAY, PRESIDENT THEODORE ROOSEVELT

President Theodore Roosevelt was born on this day in 1858.

1. Investigate and report on the life and contributions of this president

FIRST SUBWAY OPENS

Also on this day in 1904 the first subway which proved practical started operating. It ran from the Brooklyn Bridge to mid-town Manhattan, New York.

1. Subways are one means of public transportation in large cities. Make a study of the transportation system which exists in your city or area. Decide whether the present system is adequate or inadequate. Explain in writing the reasons for your decision and suggest ways for improving the system.

STATUE OF LIBERTY DEDICATED

In 1886 on Bedloe Island in New York Harbor, the famous Statue of Liberty was dedicated.

1. Investigate the history of this famous statue and write a paper based on your findings.
2. To the thousands of immigrants who left their homes to seek new lives in the U.S., the Statue of Liberty was a symbol of hope for a better life. Investigate the history of immigration to this country beginning with the turn of the century (1900) and write a paper based on your findings.
3. The word "liberty" has different meanings to different people. What does it mean to you? Write a paper explaining your personal viewpoint.

SIR WALTER RALEIGH EXECUTED

In 1618 Sir Walter Raleigh was executed in London, England. He was charged with treason.

1. Investigate the life and contributions of this man and report on your findings.

STOCK MARKET COLLAPSES

On this day in 1929 the New York Stock Exchange collapsed resulting in many fortunes being wiped out and marking the beginning of the depression of the 30's.

1. Investigate and report on how it is possible for the New York stock market to collapse. Define in your report the meaning of stock, bond, stock exchange, recession, and depression.

2. If you have a parent, other relative, friend or neighbor who lived through the depression of the 30's, interview that person to find out what sacrifices they and their family made. How did they live through his trying period; were they employed; what were their weekly wages; what did they do for entertainment,? Write a report based on your interview.

"WAR OF THE WORLDS" PANIC

In 1938 Orson Wells caused a national panic by producing a radio program called "War of the Worlds." This program seemed so real that people listening actually believed that the reported invasion of Earth by people from Mars was really happening. Thousands of people became hysterical because they thought the news bulletins on the radio program were real.

1. *War of the Worlds* is one of many excellent science fiction stories. Read a science fiction story and report on your reading using the form your teacher requests.

2. Can you write a good science fiction story? Here are a few beginning sentences to help you start thinking. Use one of these or make up one of your own.

   The headline read: Plutonians Declare War on Earth.
   He was all alone when he first saw the blue flash of light.
   Captain Vegas landed his ship on the soft desert of Mercurian while hundreds of yellow eyes hidden behind rocks anxiously watched.

3. From time to time the news media carry reports of sightings of U.F.O's (Unidentified Flying Objects) or, as they are commonly called, flying saucers. Investigate the topic of U.F.O's and report on your findings. Include in your paper a statement of your personal belief or disbelief in flying saucers and life on other planets.

AMERICAN EDUCATION WEEK

Every year a week in October (usually from October 26 to November 1) is designated as American Education Week. During this time most schools hold open house and invite parents and members of the community to visit the schools and observe the facilities, student work, and classes in session, etc.

1. Investigate and report on the history of the American system of education.
2. Write a paper contrasting the American educational system with that of another country of your choice. Conclude your paper with a statement explaining whether, if you had a choice, you would go to school in another country or remain where you are. Give reasons for your answer.

CONGRATULATIONS, NEVADA

In 1864 Nevada was admitted into the Union.

1. Identify this state on a map of the U.S. Make a free-hand drawing on a large piece of paper of the state's outline. Indicate on your map the following: capital city, principal cities, principal rivers or lakes, historical landmarks, if any, mountains, deserts, and other items of interest. Identify references used.
2. Construct a collage indicating this state's major industries. You may wish to place your collage within the boundaries of the state's outline on a U.S. map or use your imagination in creating the outline of the state by piecing together various materials. Your collage may contain actual examples of the products of this state, or drawings or pictures of the products, or a combination of all three. Identify references used.

TRICK OR TREAT

The 31st of October is Halloween Day.

1. When families from the Old World came to this country, they brought many of the customs, beliefs, and superstitions associated with Halloween with them. Try to find out what

some of them were and if they are still observed in modern-day Halloween activities. Write a report based on your findings.

2. Trick or Treating is a popular modern-day custom. To most it is a fun day but to others it is an opportunity for revenge or "to get even." Using any medium you wish, prepare a poster called "Halloween Matters and Manners" illustrating things that should and should not be done while out trick or treating as a courtesy to others.
3. Read a spooky short story or novel and report on your reading using the form your teacher suggests.
4. Here is the beginning of a Halloween poem. See if you can finish it. It can be as long as you like. Try to keep the rhyming pattern.

> It was on one cold, clear Halloween night
> That I had a very bad fright
> For sailing in the sky came a broom bearing a witch
> And I was so startled that I fell into a ditch.
>
> But quickly I got up and continued on my walk
> Until I came upon a lively fellow made of corn stalk...

5. Consult an anthology and read several Halloween poems. Select your favorite for illustration using the medium of your choice. Present a copy of the poem in your best handwriting along with your picture.

October Game of the Month

Dial-A-Word

No. of Players: 2, 3, or 4
Grade level: elementary
Materials Required: One gameboard for *each* player (see diagram and directions for making the board page 66), pencil and paper for writing, one kitchen timer.
Rules:
1. Each player may turn one or more of the wheels to obtain any setting on the board desired. Once a setting has been selected, the

game begins when one of the players sets the timer for an agreed upon length of time, such as 5, 10, or 15 minutes.

2. When the player setting the clock says, "Go" all players begin copying down on paper all the four letter words that can be made by reading down the letters in each segment of the four concentric circles. Once the game has started, no player may move any of the wheels on his gameboard. Each player must try to get as many four letter words from the particular dial setting he has decided upon as he can. Players should be careful to use only those four letter combinations which actually form words found in a standard dictionary.

3. At the end of the time period, the players exchange papers. Each player examines the word list written by the other player to determine whether or not all words listed are real words which can be found in a dictionary. Each player should feel free to consult a dictionary to verify the existence of any questionable words appearing on the list. The list of words is then totaled and the paper returned to the player. One point is scored for each word on the list but two points are deducted for each word not found in the dictionary. If time permits play continues with other rounds and the winner is the player with the most points when play stops.

Variations:
1. Play Vocabulary Dial-A-Word. Play as described above but extend the time period to 15, 20, or more minutes for each round. After a player has selected a setting on the dials and the timer is set, play begins with each player copying down on his paper all the four letter words which can be made by reading down the letters in each segment. Next to each word copied the player must define the word. When time is up, players exchange papers and check the accuracy of the words and definitions using the dictionary whenever necessary. One point is given for each word and each correct definition. A penalty of two is deducted from the total score for each word listed which does not appear in a dictionary and for each definition which is incorrect. The teacher will act as judge to settle disputes. Play continues in this way for several rounds, and the winner is the one with the most points when play is terminated.

2. Play Vocabulary Dial-A-Word Play-off. Play as explained in Number 1 above but involve the entire class. Divide the children into pairs. Have the children play against each other. Record the

winner of each pair. Then have the winners of these pairs play each other. Continue this process of "play offs" until a "vocabulary champ" is determined.

DIRECTIONS FOR MAKING DIAL-A-WORD GAME

For each player construct four concentric circles equal or similar to the diagram below. Each segment of the four circles must be 10°.

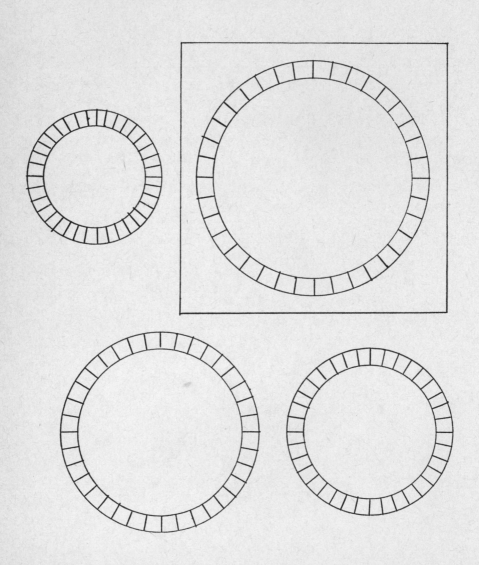

Copy the letters in each segment of the four circles. Then cut out the circles and place them together with the smallest circle on the top, the second smallest next, etc. Secure the three circles to the fourth circle, which is drawn on a larger piece of cardboard to act as backing, with a machine screw and nut or small paper fastener. Each of the top three circles should turn easily and independently of the other circles.

The following letters should be placed in the largest (outside) circle, one letter to each segment, in the following order:
G, W, T, L, D, E, R, E, R, L, E, W, Y, E, T, P, L, D, E, H, G, R, L, M, E, D, R, T, E, F, T, F, E, P, M, N

The following letters should be placed in the second largest circle, one letter to each segment, in the following order:
S, F, D, A, R, E, N, O, R, L, I, G, U, R, A, I, L, O, A, C, S, M, I, N, T, S, N, A, L, I, N, R, A, R, V, L

The following letters should be placed in the third largest circle, one letter to each segment, in the following order:
O, A, E, A, I, O, E, U, I, L, A, H, O, R, A, I, O, A, O, A, E, A, O, L, R, I, O, U, A, E, I, A, I, E, U, R

The following letters should be placed in the smallest circle, one letter to each segment, in the following order:
N, G, T, B, S, P, H, W, G, L, R, S, F, W, T, G, C, H, V, S, D, Y, B, N, T, S, P, D, L, M, J, S, B, C, R, D

Chapter Three

November

1

STAMP ACT PROTEST

In 1765 colonists protested the Stamp Act by flying flags at half mast.

1. The colonists were upset by this act and referred to it as "taxation without representation." Pretend you were an editor of a newspaper during this period of time. Write an editorial giving your opinion on taxation without representation.

MONEY ORDERS INTRODUCED

In 1864 the Post Office Department introduced the money order system.

1. Money orders are one means of sending money safely and conveniently through the mail. They are a form of paper money. Make a poster showing examples of all forms of paper money: currency, money orders, checks, credit cards, etc.
2. Investigate and report on articles or things which in the past have been used as money or make a display of the actual articles accompanied by a brief explanation.

INVISIBLE RABBIT IS HIT

In 1944 a play about an invisible rabbit called *Harvey* opened in New York City and was later awarded the Pulitzer Drama Award.

1. Read a short play and write a summary describing the plot, main characters, and your personal reaction to the play, or use a form which your teacher suggests.
2. Investigate and report on the history of the Pulitzer Prize and explain in your paper to whom this prize is awarded and state some of the recent winners.
3. If possible, attend the live performance of a play. Write a summary describing the plot, main characters, and your personal reactions, or use a form which your teacher suggests.

HAPPY BIRTHDAY, PRESIDENT POLK

In 1795 President James K. Polk was born.
1. Investigate and report on the life and contributions of this president.

HAPPY BIRTHDAY, PRESIDENT HARDING

In 1865 President Warren G. Harding was born.
1. Investigate and report on the life and contributions of this president.

CONGRATULATIONS, NORTH AND SOUTH DAKOTA

Also on this day in 1889 North and South Dakota were admitted into the Union.
1. (Use the activities suggested for the admission of Nevada, on page 63.)

POUND BUTTER COSTS 8 CENTS

On this day in 1837 housewives in Illinois were concerned about the high cost of living because a pound of butter cost 8 cents, a dozen eggs 6 cents, beef 3 cents a pound, pork 2 cents a pound, coffee 20 cents a pound, and sugar 10 cents a pound.
1. Today housewives all over the country are still concerned about the high cost of food. Make a poster illustrating the high cost of eating. You may wish to show the prices of

various food items from year to year, or to compare the present day prices for the items mentioned to the price of these items back in 1837.

2. A housewife who is wise can beat the high cost of eating through careful planning. Find out how much your family spends weekly on food. Consult the person(s) in your family who prepares the menus and shops for the food. Prepare a weekly menu which your family thinks is realistic. Estimate the cost of each item on the menu. Accompany the family shopper and determine the actual cost. Also determine the total cost per day for feeding your family and the total cost per week. Write a report based on your findings.

3. One way to save money when shopping for groceries is to watch the food ads and shop for sale items. Prepare a weekly menu for your family. You may wish to consult with the member of your family who usually prepares the menus. Prepare a shopping list of all items needed for the weekly menu. Using the current grocery store ads and sale circulars, indicate the store and sales prices of each item on your list. Write a concluding statement indicating which store(s) should be used that particular week for shopping for the weekly menu.

4

HAPPY BIRTHDAY, WILL ROGERS

A famous American humorist, actor, and author, Will Rogers, was born in 1879.

1. Investigate and report on the life and contributions of this entertainer.
2. Will Rogers enjoyed telling jokes. Compile a collection of your favorite jokes in booklet form. You may wish to illustrate some of the jokes.
3. Write a short humorous story or read one written by someone else. Report on your reading in the form suggested by your teacher.
4. Will Rogers wrote several books in which he commented on life and politics with his dry humor. Try your hand at writing a short humorous commentary about some aspect of your life.

AUTOMOBILE PATENTED

In 1895 a patent was granted to George Selden for his invention of the automobile.
1. What would your life be like without the invention of the automobile? Write a paper entitled *"If There Were No Cars."*
2. Investigate and report on the history of the automobile, including its most recent developments and prospects for the future.

6

ELECTION DAY

The Tuesday after the first Monday in November is Election Day. In some states this day is a legal holiday. It may not always fall on November 6.
1. Although voting is a privilege and a responsibility of all citizens, many people do not exercise this right. Conduct a poll of at least 25 people of voting age to determine whether they voted in the last election (either federal, state, or local); if they did not try to find out why. Write a report summarizing the results of your poll and the reasons given by people for not voting.
2. Using whatever medium you wish, prepare a campaign poster for someone who is currently running for an office at either the local, state, or national level. Your poster should indicate the merits of your candidate and try to persuade others to vote for him.
3. In addition to voting for candidates for various offices, sometimes people are asked to vote on referendums, constitutional amendments, or other issues of federal, state, or local significance. Is there such an issue in your area which will be voted on during the next election. If so, pretend you are the editor of a newspaper and have been asked to write an editorial stating your opinion and trying to persuade others to your way of thinking. Make your editorial brief and concise

REPUBLICAN ELEPHANT BORN

In 1874 the first cartoon showing an elephant as a symbol of the Republican Party appeared in *Harper's Weekly*.
1. Make a collection of symbol cartoons which show the Republican elephant or Democratic donkey. Write a brief explanation of each cartoon.
2. Write a report describing the history of either the Republican or Democratic party.

FIRST WOMEN'S COLLEGE FOUNDED

In 1837 the first college exclusively for women, Mt. Holyoke Female Seminary, was founded in Massachusetts.
1. Investigate and report on the history of women's education in this country.

CONGRATULATIONS, MONTANA

In 1889 Montana was admitted into the Union.
(Same as #1 and #2 for Nevada, p. 63)

SADIE HAWKINS DAY

A day set aside for unmarried girls to openly pursue and possibly catch husbands called Sadie Hawkins Day was introduced in 1938 by cartoonist, Al Capp, creator of the comic strip, Li'l Abner.
1. Write a short "Sadie Hawkins" poem or story.
2. Here is the beginning of a Sadie Hawkins poem. Finish the poem adding as many lines as you wish. Try to maintain the same rhyme pattern.

> There once was a young girl called Sadie Hawkins by name,
> Who decided it was high time to start playing the game
> Of trying to catch a fellow for her to marry

And she cared not what his name, be it Tom, Dick, or Harry.

NORTHEASTERN U. S. IN THE DARK

In 1965 there was a massive power failure which involved 80,000 square miles in the northeastern part of the country. Thirty million people were in the dark for from two to 13 hours.
1. Write a short story, fiction or nonfiction, about a power failure you experienced.

CONGRESS AUTHORIZES U. S. MARINES

In 1775 the Continental Congress authorized the establishment of the U. S. Marine Corp.
1. If you are interested in the Marines or another branch of the military service as a possible career, investigate and report on the opportunities available in that particular branch of service. Indicate the training programs, education, salary, benefits, etc.
2. Write a brief history of the Marine Corps or another branch of military service in which you have an interest.

"POLLYANNA" POPULAR

In 1914 the "pollyanna" was very popular because of a book written by Eleanor H. Porter.
1. Read Ms. Porter's book and write a report in the form your teacher suggests.
2. Anyone who is eternally cheerful and always looks at the bright side of life could be called a "pollyanna." Do you know of anyone like this? If you do, write a paper entitled the "The Pollyanna I Know" and describe fully this person.

CONGRATULATIONS, WASHINGTON

In 1889 the state of Washington was admitted into the Union.
(Same as #1 and #2 for Nevada, p. 63)

ARMISTICE SIGNED ENDING WORLD WAR I

In 1918 an agreement was signed between the Allied and Central Powers marking the end of World War I. In 1938 President Franklin Roosevelt signed a law making November 11 Armistice Day, a day to honor our veterans of war. It has recently been called Veterans Day.

1. Although this special day has been set aside for Americans to honor those who died while serving their country, many Americans think of this day as just another holiday. Using any medium you wish, make a poster which could be placed in a local store window that will awaken those Americans who do not observe this holiday to remember the honoring of the war dead. With permission, place your poster in a business establishment window for others to see.

BLACK BLIZZARD?

In 1933 the "Great Black Blizzard," a big dust storm laid thousands of acres of land in the Great Plains to waste. Many people were forced to leave their homes in search of fertile land and a new way of making a living.

1. Read a short story or novel about a migrant family. Write a report summarizing your reading in the form your teacher suggests.
2. Wind is one form of land erosion. Investigate and report on the topic of erosion. Include in your paper an explanation of what erosion is, how it can be prevented, and if possible, include pictures showing examples of different kinds erosion.

"HAIL COLUMBIA"

Joseph Hopkinson, author of the patriotic song, "Hail Columbia," was born in 1770.

1. Investigate and report on the life and contributions of this song writer.
2. Make a tape recording for listening by your classmates of patriotic songs, including "Hail Columbia." It may be an original recording showing your musical talents or music taken from recorded sources. Include a brief explanation or history about each excerpt on the tape.

3. Obtain a copy of the lyrics of "Hail Columbia." Using any medium, prepare an illustration bearing the same title as the song.
4. Write an essay entitled: American Patriotism: Present or Absent?

"THE SHEIK"

In 1921 the motion picture, "The Sheik," starring Rudolph Valentino, was released, and women started swooning over his masculinity.
1. Investigate and report on the life and contributions of this matinee idol of the past.
2. Construct a collage entitled "Movie Idols: Past and Present."
3. When "The Sheik" was made, Hollywood motion picture studios were beginning their climb to success. Today many of the major motion picture studios have been sold, destroyed, or converted into making pictures for television. Investigate and report on the topic: The Rise and Fall of Hollywood Motion Picture Studios.

SIT-DOWN STRIKE

In 1933 the first sit-down strike in the U. S. occurred at the Hormel Packing Plant in Austin, Minnesota.
1. Use the concept of a sit-down strike by either students or teachers as the main plot of a short story you compose.

"HORSE CAR"

The first street car in the world appeared on the streets of New York City in 1832. People referred to it as a "horse car" because it was drawn along the tracks by two horses.
1. Using any medium, prepare an illustration of this first street car. Consult a history book if necessary and try to make your illustration as accurate as possible.

MOBY DICK PUBLISHED

The book, *Moby Dick*, written by Herman Melville was published in 1851.
1. Read this book or an adaptation of it and report on your reading in a form suggested by your teacher.
2. Using any medium you wish, prepare an illustration of one or more scenes from this classic story.

PHILIPPINES GET PRESIDENT

In 1935 the first president of this country was inaugurated.
1. Investigate and report on this country. Include in your report the major cities, capital city, major industries, brief history, culture, and customs of the people.

ARTICLES OF CONFEDERATION ADOPTED

In 1777 the Articles of Confederation were adopted and submitted to the states for approval.
1. Investigate and report on the history behind this document.

LEAGUE OF NATIONS BEGINS

In 1920 the first meeting of the League of Nations was called to order in Geneva, Switzerland. The U. S., however, was not part of this organization.
1. Investigate the history of the League of Nations. Write a paper based on your findings. Be sure to explain why the U. S. did not belong to this organization.
2. Pretend you were an editor of a newspaper in 1920. Decide whether or not the U. S. should join the League of Nations and write a short editorial stating your opinion and reasons.

SHERMAN STARTS MARCH TO THE SEA

In 1864 Union General William Sherman began his "March to the Sea" through the state of Georgia.

1. Investigate the life and contributions of this general and report your findings.
2. Read a short story or novel about the Civil War. Write a summary of your reading in the form your teacher suggests.

CONGRATULATIONS, OKLAHOMA

In 1907 the State of Oklahoma was admitted to the Union.
(Same as #1 and #2 for Nevada, p. 63)

FEDERAL RESERVE BANKS OPEN

In 1914 the 12 Federal Reserve Banks were opened to supervise banking in the U. S.
1. Write a short report explaining the history, need, and functions of the federal reserve system.
2. Most people think of banks as a place to save money. But, banks offer other services. Visit several neighborhood banks and determine exactly what services they offer customers. Write a report summarizing your findings.

CONGRESS IS HOME

In 1800 the Congress convened in Washington for the first time using the north wing of the capital building.
1. Make a poster or bulletin board display of important buildings in Washington. Label each appropriately. Also indicate the functions performed by each of these buildings.

GOMPERS ORGANIZES UNION

In 1881 Samuel Gompers organized the Federation of Organized Trades and Labor Unions, an organization which was a forerunner of the American Federation of Labor Unions.
1. Investigate and report on the life and contributions of this union organizer.
2. If you know of relatives, friends, or neighbors who are union members, interview them to determine what benefits they receive from their union, dues they must pay, advantages and disadvantages of union membership. Write a report sum-

marizing the results of your interview. Try to interview as many different union members as you can.

18

NATION DIVIDED INTO TIME ZONES

In 1883 the U. S. adopted Standard Time and divided the country into time zones.
1. Free-hand draw or trace a large map of the U. S., including Hawaii and Alaska. Indicate time zone dividing lines and the time difference between each.
2. Today people fly quickly from one time zone to another. Such flights may result in "jet lag." Investigate and report on the topic of jet lag. Explain what happens to the human body during a jet lag condition and how people can reduce its effects. If you have ever experienced jet lag, indicate your own feelings.

PANAMA GETS INDEPENDENCE

In 1903 Panama and the U. S. signed a treaty recognizing the Republic of Panama as independent and granting the U. S. a ten-mile strip of land for construction of the canal.
1. Investigate and report on the history and advantages of the Panama Canal.
2. Investigate and report on the Republic of Panama. Include its major industries, population, customs and culture, size, etc.

19

HAPPY BIRTHDAY, PRESIDENT GARFIELD

In 1831 President James A. Garfield was born.
1. Investigate and report on the life and contributions of this president.

GETTYSBURG ADDRESS A FLOP

In 1863 President Lincoln dedicated a cemetery at Gettysburg, Pennsylvania. His dedication speech was only 10 sentences long. It was delivered in two minutes and was considered to be insignificant at the time. Today it is considered a classic.

1. Read the famous Gettysburg address. Explain in your own words the meaning of this famous speech.

CARRIE NATION SELLS HATCHETS

In 1903 the famous prohibitionist, Carrie Nation, created a disturbance in the gallery of the Senate by trying to make a speech and sell replicas of her famous hatchet.
1. Investigate and report on the life and contributions of this famous woman.
2. The prohibitionist movement attempted to outlaw drinking of alcohol. Investigate to find out the effects of alcohol on the body and write a report based on your findings. Include in your paper your opinion about whether drinking should be outlawed.

20

PHOTOGRAPHS REQUIRED FOR PASSPORTS

The State Department announced in 1914 that American citizens requesting passports must submit a photograph along with other official papers.
1. Prepare a photograph display on posterboard or the bulletin board which tells a story. Caption each picture.
2. If photography is one of your hobbies, prepare a written or oral report explaining various aspects of photography with which you are familiar.

CUBAN QUARANTINE LIFTED

President Kennedy lifted the naval quarantine of Cuba in 1962.
1. Investigate and report on the significance of this historical event. Speculate on what might have happened if the U. S. had not imposed a quarantine when it did.

21

TALKING MACHINE INVENTED

In 1877 Thomas Edison announced he had invented the talking machine or phonograph.
1. Investigate the life and contributions of this famous inventor and report on your findings.

2. Inventors usually patent their inventions. Write a paper describing the purpose and length of a patent and how one should go about obtaining one. Explain the difference between patents and copyrights.
3. Using whatever medium you wish, and a large 9-inch clean paper plate create a commemorative plate in honor of Thomas Edison and his many inventions.

22

S. O. S. ADOPTED

In 1906 the International Radio Telegraphic Convention adopted the S. O. S. distress signal as a warning to be used by disabled ships.
1. Compose a short story entitled S. O. S.

"CHINA CLIPPER" CARRIES MAIL

In 1935 an airplance called the "China Clipper" left San Francisco for the first trans-Pacific airmail flight. It traveled 8,000 miles making stops in Honolulu, Midway, Wake, Guam, and arriving in Manila. The trip took 7 days.
1. Free-hand draw or trace a map indicating the route of the China Clipper.

23

HAPPY BIRTHDAY, PRESIDENT PIERCE

In 1804 President Franklin Pierce was born.
1. Investigate the life and contributions of this president and report on your findings.

FOOD RATIONING ENDS

In 1945 all food rationing except sugar came to an end in the U. S.
1. Interview several people who lived during the period of food rationing during World War II. Try to find out what it was like to live this way, what foods were rationed, how people coped and adjusted to this. Prepare a written report summarizing the results of your interviews.
2. Recently there has been talk of rationing another commodity—fuel. Such rationing may not necessarily be

needed if people will voluntarily conserve their use of fuel. Using any medium you wish, construct a poster which could be placed in a local store window reminding people of ways to conserve fuel. With permission, place your poster in a business window for others to view.
3. Pretend you are the editor of a newspaper who has been asked to write an editorial on rationing. Decide on your position. You are either for rationing of fuel or against it. Prepare an editorial trying to persuade others to your way of thinking. Be sure to give reasons for your position.

HAPPY BIRTHDAY, PRESIDENT TAYLOR

In 1784 the 12th President, Zachary Taylor, was born.
1. Investigate and report on the life and contributions of this president.

WOMEN ORGANIZE TO GET THE VOTE

In 1869 women representing 21 states gathered in Cleveland to organize the American Women's Suffrage Association. The leader of this group was Lucy Stone and the main speaker, Julia Ward Howe.
1. Investigate and report on the women's suffrage movement. Include in your paper the leaders of this movement and at what point in history women were finally given the vote.

FIRST WOMAN FLIES ACROSS COUNRY

In 1930 for the first time in history, a woman, Ruth Nichols, started out on a transcontinental flight across the U. S. Her flight took 7 days.
1. Investigate and report on this or another famous woman flyer and her contributions.

GOLD GUINEAS SUNK IN NEW YORK HARBOR

In 1780 a British ship, Hussar, sank in New York Harbor carrying 900,000 gold guineas, and no record to date has been found of its recovery

1. Compose a short story using the above information as the main plot.

DINNER FOR TWO COSTS 25 CENTS

One of New York's finest restaurants, Delmonico's, reported that a meal of soup, steak, coffee, and half a pie cost 12 cents in 1834; dinner for two cost 25 cents. The extra penny was for a second cup of coffee.

1. Survey five or more neighborhood restaurant menus to determine how much the same meal, for one and for two, would cost today. If more than one type of soup, steak, or pie is listed, use the lowest priced one for your survey. Prepare a chart and summary of the results of the survey. Do not consider other things such as quality of food, atmosphere, etc. Base your report strictly on price.

FIRST FOOTBALL GAME BROADCAST

In 1920 the first radio broadcast of a football game was made by WTAW of College Station, Texas.

1. Prepare a tape recording of your own step by step description of an activity you are viewing in person. Keep in mind that your audience does not see the same things you are seeing. The audience must rely upon your descriptions. You will be their eyes.

HAPPY BIRTHDAY, MR. HARVARD

On this day in 1635 the founder of a famous university, John Harvard, was born.

1. If your future plans include a college education, investigate the history of Harvard University or another college or university of your choice. Report on your findings. Include in your report an estimate of what your college education will cost.

ALICE IN WONDERLAND

In 1864 a math teacher at Oxford University, England sent a Christmas gift to Alice, a 12-year old girl and daughter of a clergyman. His gift was a handwritten script of a story he had written especially for Alice called *Alice's Adventures Underground*. This later became known as *Alice in Wonderland*, and the teacher took the pen name of Lewis Carroll.

1. Read this famous book and write a report on your reading in a form suggested by your teacher.
2. Using any medium you wish, illustrate one or more scenes from this famous story.
3. If you have a good imagination, try writing your own version of *Blank* (insert your name in the blank) *in Wonderland* (or use another word such as candyland, automobile land, model train land, etc.)

THANKSGIVING PROCLAIMED

The fourth Thursday in November is designated by presidential proclamation as Thanksgiving Day.

1. Investigate and report on the first Thanksgiving held by the Pilgrims in the fall of 1621.
2. Using any medium you wish, illustrate the first Pilgrim Thanksgiving. You will want to read about this event before starting your illustration. Try to make your picture as authentic as possible.
3. Over the years many objects have come to be associated with the celebration of Thanksgiving, such as turkeys, pumpkin pie, cranberries, etc. Using any medium you wish, make a poster or mobile entitled Symbols of Modern-day Thanksgiving. If you decide to make a mobile, use a coat hanger as your base.
4. Give serious thought to what has happened to you and your family this past year. Write a paper describing the things for which you and your family should be thankful.

MAGELLAN ENTERS PACIFIC OCEAN

On this day in 1520 explorer Ferdinand Magellan entered the Pacific Ocean on his trip around the world.

1. Investigate and report on the life and contributions of this famous explorer.

COFFEE RATIONING STARTED

In 1942 the rationing of coffee started in the U. S.

1. Recently there has been talk among leaders of government and business that the possibility of rationing gasoline and fuel oil for heating homes may become a necessity in the future. Consider what this would mean to you and your family if gas and home heating oil were rationed. What sacrifices would you and your family have to make? How would you and your family's life style change? What unnecessary automobile trips might have to be eliminated? How might your family conserve fuel for heating and cooking? Write a paper explaining your thoughts.

COCOANUT GROVE PANIC

In 1942 a fire in a Boston night club, the Cocoanut Grove, resulted in the death of almost 500 people because they panicked and stampeded in their attempt to get out.

1. Your school probably has many practice fire drills throughout the year to avoid the kind of panic which resulted in so many deaths in the Boston night club fire. Using any medium you choose, make a poster or bulletin board illustration of rules to remember during a school fire drill.
2. Many families are also holding family fire drills to avoid panic if a fire should break out in their home. If your family does not have a fire escape plan and fire routine, discuss this matter with your family and together set up your fire drill routine. Describe in writing your family's fire drill routine and the responsibilities of each member of the family, if a fire should occur.

"BIG THREE" MEET

In 1943 President Franklin D. Roosevelt met Premier Joseph Stalin of the Soviet Union and Prime Minister Winston Churchill of England to discuss the invasion of western Europe during World War II.

1. Investigate and report on the life and contributions of one or more of these three famous leaders.

29

KING TUT'S TOMB DISCOVERED

In 1922 Lord Carnarvon of England and his American assistant, Howard Carter, discovered the tomb of Egyptian King Tutankhamen.
1. Investigate the early civilization of Egypt and write a report on your findings. Explain how the Egyptians lived, the monuments they created, and their beliefs associated with death.
2. The Egyptians constructed large tombs called pyramids for the burial of their royalty. Investigate the topic of pyramids and write a report based on your findings.
3. The ancient Egyptian civilization is famous for its mummies. Investigate and report on this topic.
4. Investigate and report on the legend of King Tutankhamen.

BYRD FLIES OVER SOUTH POLE

In 1929 Lt. Commander Richard E. Byrd and his three-man crew were the first people to fly over the South Pole.
1. Investigate and report on the life and contributions of this modern-day explorer.

30

HAPPY BIRTHDAY, MR. TWAIN

In 1835 Samuel Langhorne Clemens, who later assumed the pen name of Mark Twain, was born.
1. Investigate and report on the life and contributions of this famous author.
2. Read one or more of his stories and report in writing on your reading following the form suggested by your teacher.
3. Using any medium you wish, illustrate one or more scenes from one of Mr. Twain's novels.
4. Try writing a short adventure story in which you imagine yourself as the main character, Tom Sawyer or Huck Finn.

November Game of the Month
Beat the Clock Math

Number of players: 2

Grade level: elementary

Materials: Card deck composed of 3 x 5 cards on which a variety of math problems appropriate to grade level are written on one side with the solution on the other side; two stop watches; scratch paper; pencils

Rules:

1. At the beginning of the game the card deck should be shuffled and placed between the two players. One stop watch should be placed in front of each player, and each player should have scratch paper and pencils to use in figuring solutions to problems.

2. Play begins by a player turning over a card from the deck to reveal the problem. As this is done both stop watches should be started. Players then proceed to figure out a solution. As soon as a player has an answer he must stop his stopwatch and wait for the other player to do the same. Players should figure solutions independently of each other and not allow answers to be seen during the computation process. When both watches have been stopped and both players have reached a solution to the problem, the card is turned over to reveal the answer. If both players have the correct answer, the player who finished first scores points for each second by which he beat his opponent. For example, if player A took 30 seconds to finish and Player B took 20 seconds, player B gets 10 points, assuming both players had the correct answer. If only one player is correct, no matter how long it took that player to get the solution, the player with the correct answer scores points equal to the number of seconds it took him to obtain the solution. If neither player is correct, it is considered a "draw" and no points are earned by any player. Play continues in this way until the card deck has been used up or time has run out. The player with the most points at end of play wins. Note: it is recommended that students of equal ability be paired as opponents.

Variations:

1. Play as directed above but if both players do not get the right answer, impose a penalty as follows: Each player deducts from his score points equal to the number of seconds it took him to work the problem.

2. Play as above but work in teams of 2, 3, or 4 players on each team. The first person to get the correct answer on each team scores for his team the number of seconds by which he beat the other team in getting an answer.

Chapter Four

December

$\boxed{1}$

NO ELECTORAL MAJORITY

In 1824 a problem developed when none of the presidential candidates received an electoral majority.

    1. Investigate to find out how this problem was resolved and who was eventually elected. Write a report of your findings.

INNOVATION IN BANKING—CHRISTMAS CLUB

The first "Christmas Club," a new thing in banking, was introduced in Carlisle, Pennsylvania in 1909.

    1. Today many banks and savings and loan institutions still have Christmas Clubs whose purpose is to encourage people to save a certain amount every week or specific period of time to provide money for Christmas shopping. Using the medium of your choice, create a poster or bulletin board display entitled "Tips for Saving." Your display should show different ways to save money safely.

GAS STATION IN STABLE?

Until 1913 people who drove cars had to purchase gas in livery stables and garages. On this day, however, the first drive-in gasoline station opened for business in Pittsburgh, Pennsylvania. Today gas stations have changed since they first opened.

    1. Make a survey of several gas stations in your local area to determine what services are offered, the type and price of gas,

inducements for buying (stamps, coupons, discounts, etc). Write a report summarizing the results of the survey. Show gas prices in graph or chart form.

BOYS TOWN FOUNDED

In 1917 Father Edward Flannagan founded Boys Town, a community which offered shelter for homeless boys and was run by the boys themselves.
1. Investigate and report on the history of this famous town. You might wish to write to Boys Town and request their assistance in providing information for your report.

2

MONROE DOCTRINE DEVELOPED

In 1823 President James Monroe read an annual message to Congress which was later called the Monroe Doctrine.
1. Investigate and report on what the Monroe Doctrine said in your own words and explain why it was considered politically important.

FORD INTRODUCES MODEL "A"

In 1927 Henry Ford introduced his Model A car to the public. This car was to replace the older Model T. It cost $385 and came in different colors whereas the Model T came only in black.
1. Make a display of antique cars using models, pictures, drawings, etc. Write a brief description of each model in your display.
2. What do you think cars of the future will be like? Write a report explaining your opinions. You might wish to write to the major automobile manufacturers to request information for your report. If possible, try to include some pictures or drawings of future cars.

THE BIRTH OF THE ATOMIC AGE

This day is considered to be the birthday of the Atomic Age. In 1942 the first self-sustaining nuclear chain reaction was demonstrated at the University of Chicago. Much of the credit for the development of the atomic bomb belongs to an Italian physicist, Enrico Fermi.

1. Investigate and report on the life and contributions of this Italian scientist.
2. The atomic bomb was used during World War II. It was dropped on two Japanese cities, Hiroshima and Nagasaki. Investigate and report on the effects of the bombings on these two cities.
3. Investigate and report on modern-day uses of atomic and nuclear energy.

3

CONGRATULATIONS, ILLINOIS

In 1818 Illinois joined the Union as the 21st state.
(Same as #1 and #2 for Nevada, p. 63)

JEFFERSON DAVIS GOES ON TRIAL

The trial of the former President of the Confederacy, Jefferson Davis, began in 1868. Mr. Davis was charged with treason.
1. Investigate and report on the life and contributions of this Confederate leader.

4

WASHINGTON'S FAREWELL

In 1783 George Washington gave a tearful farewell when he resigned his commission as Commander in Chief of the Continental Army.
1. Using any medium you wish, illustrate this moment in history.

FIRST PRESIDENT VISITS FOREIGN COUNTRY

In 1918 Woodrow Wilson became the first President to visit a foreign country while holding office when he sailed for France to attend the Peace Conference at Versailles.
1. Investigate and report on this President's life and contributions.

ROOSEVELT ATTENDS CAIRO CONFERENCE

In 1943 President Roosevelt attended the second Cairo conference where he met with Prime Minister Winston Churchill and President Ismet Inona of Turkey.

    1. Investigate and report on the life and contributions of one or more of these leaders.

HAPPY BIRTHDAY, PRESIDENT VAN BUREN

In 1782 the eighth President, Martin Van Buren, was born.

    1. Investigate and report on the life and contributions of this president.

GOLD RUSH BEGINS

President Polk, while delivering his yearly message to the Congress, confirmed that gold had been discovered in California. This led to the Gold Rush of 1848-49.

    1. Write a paper describing the gold rush period of our country's history. Explain in your paper where the gold rush occurred, why people were so interested in acquiring gold, and why even today gold still has high value.

PROHIBITION ENDS

In 1933 national prohibition came to an end when the State of Utah was the last state to ratify the 21st amendment to the Constitution.

    1. Investigate and report on the history of the prohibition period of our country.

    2. Prohibitionists wanted the drinking of alcohol outlawed because they thought it was bad. Investigate and report on the ill effects of alcohol consumption.

A DAY FOR ST. NICHOLAS

Some religions still celebrate the feast of St Nicholas on this day. In modern times, St. Nicholas has come to be synonymous with Santa Claus.

1. Investigate and report on customs in this country and others associated with St. Nicholas.
2. Using any medium you wish, create your personal interpretation of "jolly old St. Nicholas."
3. Santa Claus is sometimes called St. Nick. Investigate and report on the origins of the legend of Santa Claus and how he came to be associated with St. Nick.
4. Compose a short Christmas story in which St. Nicholas (Santa Claus) is the main character.

DELAWARE DAY

This day is observed by citizens of Delaware as Delaware Day in honor of the anniversary of the adoption of the Constitution in 1787. Delaware was the first state to formally ratify the Constitution.

1. Using any medium of your choice and a clean 9-inch paper plate, create a commemorative plate in honor of Delaware Day.

LIBRARY DAY

The first Friday in December, Library Day, has been observed in the past in some schools in West Virginia. It does not always fall on December 7. The purpose of this day is to arouse interest in the school library and to raise money for buying new books.

1. Investigate your own school or local public library. Try to find out what is available. Using any medium you wish, create a poster which will advertise the many services and books available at this library.

PEARL HARBOR BOMBED!

In 1941 the Japanese launched a surprise attack on the U.S. installations at Pearl Harbor, Hawaii, in the Philippines, and on Wake and Guam Islands. This sneak attack resulted in the sinking of several U.S. warships, the loss of many planes, and thousands of men dead and injured. At the time the U.S. was not at war with Japan.

1. Investigate and report on the bombing of Pearl Harbor. If possible, include as part of your report an interview with someone who experienced this attack.

2. For most people who are old enough to remember World War II, the bombing of Pearl Harbor is a vivid memory. Interview several people who remember this war to find out what their reactions were to the news about Pearl Harbor and how this attack personally affected their lives. Write a report summarizing your interviews.

RECONSTRUCTION PLANS BEGIN

In 1863 President Lincoln announced his plans for reconstructing the South after the Civil War.

1. Investigate and report on Lincoln's plan for reconstruction.

U.S. DECLARES WAR ON JAPAN!

In 1941 Congress declared war on Japan thus beginning American involvement in World War II.

1. Using any medium you wish, make a World War II time line illustrating the most important events. If you wish accompany your illustration with a brief written statement about each item on your time line. Put your work on a bulletin board.

NO NEWS IS BAD NEWS

In 1962 a newspaper strike in New York City shut down all nine newspapers for 114 days.

1. Although the New York City newspapers were on strike, people could still get their news by listening to the radio or television. Suppose that all three mediums were on strike at the same time. What would it be like? How could people get news? What measures might be taken in such a time of emergency? Write a paper describing your thoughts on this subject.

CREATOR "UNCLE REMUS AND BRER RABBIT" BORN

In 1848 Joel Chandler Harris, author of the famous Uncle Remus and Brer Rabbit stories, was born.

1. Read one or more of the Uncle Remus stories and report on your reading following a format suggested by your teacher.
2. Using any medium you wish, illustrate one or more scenes from your favorite Uncle Remus stories.

FIRST CHRISTMAS SEALS GO ON SALE

In 1907 the first Christmas Seals designed by Emily Bissell of Wilmington, Delaware were placed on sale. The proceeds from the sale were to help fight the disease, tuberculosis.

1. Using any medium you wish and a large piece of paper, design a number of your own "Christmas Seals." You might wish to examine old Christmas Seals before starting this project to see what types of things are pictured on the seals.

CONGRATULATIONS, MISSISSIPPI

In 1817 Mississippi, the 20th state, was admitted into the Union. (Same as #1 and #2 for Nevada, p. 63)

SPANISH-AMERICAN WAR ENDS

In 1898 Spain signed the Treaty of Paris which ended the Spainish-American War and gave the U.S. the territories of Guam, Puerto Rico, and the Philippines.

1. Investigate and report on one or more of these territories acquired from Spain. Include in your report a brief history, major cities, capital city, population, major industries, and other points of interest.

WYOMING DAY

The legislature of Wyoming in 1935 designated this day as Wyoming Day, a time set aside to observe the history of the state.

1. Using any medium you wish and a clean 9-inch paper plate, create a commemorative plate in honor of Wyoming's history.

☐ 11

CONGRATULATIONS, INDIANA

Indiana, the 19th state, was admitted into the Union in 1816.
(Same as #1 and #2 for Nevada, p. 63)

☐ 12

FIRST "BEST SELLER"

Many publishers consider Susan Warner's novel, *The Wide, Wide World,* as the first best seller in the U. S. It was published in 1850.
  1. Have you read a book which you think is so good that it may also be a best seller? If so, report on your reading using a format suggested by your teacher.

MESSAGES ACROSS ATLANTIC

Guglielmo Marconi and his assistant successfully transmitted a message across the Atlantic Ocean in 1901.
  1. Investigate and report on the life and contributions of Mr. Marconi.

BIG GIFT

In 1955 the Ford Foundation gave one-half billion dollars to private hospitals, colleges, and medical schools.
  1. If you had a large amount of money to donate, to whom would you give the money and for what reasons? Establish a priority of ten people, institutions, or organizations that you would give money to and be sure to explain your reasons.

☐ 13

NEW ZEALAND DISCOVERED

The island of New Zealand was discovered in 1642 by Abel Tasman, a navigator from Holland.

1. Investigate and report on the life and contributions of this explorer.
2. Investigate and report on the country of New Zealand. Include in your report a brief history, its principal cities, capital city, major industries, and other facts you consider important.
3. Free-hand draw or trace a large map of New Zealand. Identify on this map the following: major cities, capital city, mountains, deserts, plains, principal rivers, lakes, and areas of the country where major industries predominate.

14

CONGRATULATIONS, ALABAMA

Alabama, the 22nd state, entered the Union in 1819.
(Same as #1 and #2 for Nevada, p. 63)

SOUTH POLE DISCOVERED

Roald Amundsen, a Norwegian explorer, discovered the South Pole in 1911.
1. Investigate and report on the life and contributions of this modern-day explorer.

MINIATURE GOLF INVENTED

Garnet Carter established a new national pastime—miniature golf in Florida, in 1929.
1. If you have ever played miniature golf and understand the game's operation, try your hand at establishing your own miniature golf course. With your teacher's permission, set up a miniature golf course in your classroom or on the playground. Use cardboard boxes of various sizes and shapes as "holes." Arrange your "holes" to form a mixture of easy and difficult shots. Use your ingenuity in converting tin cans and plastic containers of various sizes to holes, or traps. Your golf clubs can be made of yard sticks and the balls should be ping pong balls. Invite your classmates and teacher to try your course. If your teacher permits, initiate a miniature golf contest to see who is the best player in your class.

15

BILL OF RIGHTS BECOMES EFFECTIVE

In 1791 the first ten amendments to the Constitution, known as the Bill of Rights, went into effect.
1. Read the Bill of Rights and explain in your own words the meaning of each.
2. Using whatever medium you wish, create a poster or bulletin board display illustrating the Bill of Rights.

SITTING BULL KILLED

Sitting Bull, the Sioux Indian Chief, was killed in South Dakota by Federal troops in 1890.
1. Investigate the Sioux Indians' life style or that of another Indian tribe of your choice. Report on how the tribe lived in the past, how they dressed, the food they ate, how they obtained food, what they did for entertainment, etc.
2. Report on the circumstances of Sitting Bull's death.

16

BOSTON HAS A TEA PARTY

In 1773 in protest against a British tax on tea, 50 citizens of Boston participated in an event called by historians the Boston Tea Party.
1. Investigate and report on this famous event. Indicate significant events which led up to this "party."
2. Using any medium you wish, create an illustration of this famous "party." You may wish to consult a history book for a description of the event so your illustration will be authentic.

NEW YORK IS ON FIRE!

This day is the anniversary of a fire which swept over many city blocks in New York and destroyed 600 buildings in 1835.
1. Many fires can be prevented through careful observance of fire safety ules. Using any medium you wish, create a bulletin board or poster display of fire safety rules for home, school, office, or all three

TWO AIRPLANES COLLIDE

One of the worst disasters in aviation history took place in 1960 when two airplanes collided over New York Harbor killing 131 people.

1. One of the people who help prevent such accidents from happening more often than they do is the flight controller. He monitors planes from the control tower. If you think you might like to have this job as a future career, investigate and report on the controller's training, education, responsibilities, benefits, advantages, disadvantages, starting salary, working conditions, etc. If possible, include an interview with a controller to get personal reactions.
2. If you have a career interest in any other aspect of aviation, prepare a report on this career listing the same information as requested in No. 1 above.

FIRST AIRPLANE FLIGHT

In 1903 the first successful airplane flight was made by Orville and Wilbur Wright near Kitty Hawk, North Carolina.

1. Investigate and report on the life and contributions of one or both of these two flyers.
2. Assume you were a radio or television newscaster present at Kitty Hawk on this day when the first airplane flight took place. Prepare a newscast recording on tape for playing to your classmates. Keep in mind that your audience must depend on your description to be their eyes, and don't forget the five W's of news reporting.

HAPPY BIRTHDAY, MR. WHITTIER

The famous American poet, John Greenleaf Whittier, was born in 1807.

1. Consult an anthology and read several of Mr. Whittier's poems. Explain the poet's thoughts in each poem in your own words, or illustrate, using any medium you wish, one or several of the poet's ideas.

GIFT FROM CHINA—PANDA

In 1936 China sent the first giant panda to a San Francisco zoo.
1. The panda is one of many species which is in danger of becoming extinct. Write a paper entitled "Endangered Species" in which you explain which animals are in danger of becoming extinct. If possible, include pictures of some of these animals.
2. Many of those animals that were previously on the "endangered list" have actually become extinct. Write a paper entitled "Extinct Animals." If possible, include pictures of these animals and explain why they have become extinct.

19

POOR RICHARD

In 1732 Ben Franklin started publication of his *Poor Richard's Almanac*.
1. Investigate and report on the life and contributions of this famous statesman.

"THE AMERICAN CRISIS"

In 1776 Thomas Paine wrote his first installment of "The American Crisis."
1. Investigate and report on the life and contributions of this famous American patriot.

WASHINGTON CAMPS AT VALLEY FORGE

In 1777 General George Washington took about 11,000 of his men and set up camp for the winter at Valley Forge, Pennsylvania.
1. Investigate and report on the life and contributions of this famous general and first president of our country.
2. Investigate and report on this trying winter endured by Washington's troops encamped at Valley Forge. Explain in your paper what the army did for food, shelter, clothing, and recreation.

COTTON MILL STARTED

Samuel Slater, an Englishman, started the first successful American cotton mill in 1790.
1. Investigate and report on the life and contributions of this man called the Father of American Manufacturing.
2. Investigate and report on the Industrial Revolution which started in our country after the Civil War.

LOUISIANA PURCHASE

In 1803 the U.S. took possession of the Louisiana Purchase.
1. Investigate and report on the history of this famous purchase.
2. Using any medium you wish, make a large map showing the land that was acquired from France as part of this purchase. Include on your map the 1803 boundaries of this purchase and the present-day state boundaries.

BERLIN WALL OPENED

In 1963 the Berlin Wall was opened temporarily for the first time for 17 days.
1. Investigate and report on the history of the Berlin Wall.

"SNOW WHITE AND THE 7 DWARFS"

In 1937 the animated cartoon, "Snow White and the Seven Dwarfs," which was based on the Grimm's fairy tale, played for the first time. This picture was produced by Walt Disney.
1. Investigate and report on the life and contributions of this famous artist.
2. Read one or more of the Grimm's fairy tales. Report on your reading using the format suggested by your teacher. Include in this report your description of any fairy tales you have read which might be good subjects for future Disney movies.

22

DEAR SANTA CLAUS

A custom which many young children observe is writing to Santa Claus who is the giver of Christmas presents.

1. Investigate and report on this legend of Santa Claus. If possible include in your report a copy of the famous letter written by an eight-year old to the *New York Sun* asking whether there was a Santa Claus and the editor's reply.
2. Get into the spirit of Christmas by writing a short Christmas story. Here are a few beginning lines to help you get started. Use one of these or one of your own.

    Who says there's no Santa Claus?
    The Spirit of Christmas is...
    It was the night before Christmas and...
    My Most Memorable Christmas was...

3. Read the famous Christmas poem "The Night Before Christmas." Using any medium you wish, prepare a poster or bulletin board illustration of this poem. Be sure to include the lines of the poem.
4. Shopping for and wrapping Christmas presents is another task of preparing for the Christmas celebration. Pretend you are a designer who has been asked to submit several designs for Christmas wrapping paper. Use any medium you wish in preparing your designs and place each design on a separate sheet of paper.

23

GET READY FOR CHRISTMAS

In many families, this day is spent in making final preparations for the Christmas celebration.

1. If the person who does the cooking in your family makes one or more "special" things in honor of Christmas, copy down the recipes in your best handwriting and compute the cost of

each recipe. Your computations should include cost of each ingredient, total cost of preparation, and cost per serving. If desired, illustrate one or more of these recipes by using any medium you wish.

2. The custom of sending Christmas cards to friends and neighbors is one which most people follow. Using a medium of your choice, design one or more Christmas cards which you would be proud to send to your friends, relatives, and neighbors. Be sure to include an appropriate message inside the card. Try to include unusual materials or designs, verses, or unique shapes and folds to make your cards the most creative.

3. Another popular custom of the season is setting up a Christmas tree. Investigate and report on the custom of decorating a tree. Include in your report its origins, suggestions for safe decorations, and explain how "live" trees should be safely maintained and disposed of.

WAR OF 1812 ENDS

In 1814 a peace treaty was signed at Ghent, Belgium ending the War of 1812 between the U.S. and England.

1. Investigate and report on the war of 1812. Include in your paper reasons for this war, its duration, and what was gained by each side.

"RUDOLPH, THE RED NOSED REINDEER"

In 1949 the most popular new Christmas song all over the country was "Rudolph, the Red Nosed Reindeer."

1. If you like to sing or can play a musical instrument, make a live or tape presentation of popular Christmas songs.

2. Compose a story entitled, "Rudolph, the Red Nosed Reindeer" and if desired, illustrate one or more scenes from your story using any medium.

CHRISTMAS EVE

Traditionally Christmas Eve in many homes is a special day with special activities and preparations by all members of the family.

1. Explain in writing or picture form, using the medium of your choice, the activities which members of your family engage in as preparation for celebrating Christmas.
2. The Christmas season is one time when most Americans observe customs of American or ethnic origin. Explain in writing or picture form, using any medium you wish, the customs your family observes every year in celebrating Christmas. Try to trace the origins of each custom.

25

CHRISTMAS DAY

"SILENT NIGHT"

In 1818 the Christmas carol, "Silent Night, Holy Night," was sung for the first time in a village church in Austria.

1. Investigate and report on the origins or history of this and/or other famous Christmas carols.
2. If you like to sing or play a musical instrument, make a live or tape presentation of your favorite carols.
3. Investigate and report on how Christmas is celebrated in other parts of the world. Choose one or more countries and try to find out how these people celebrate.
4. Read a Christmas story. Report on your reading in a format your teacher suggests.
5. Write your own Christmas story. Try to have the story have a surprise ending.
6. Write a serious essay on Christmas entitled, "The Real Meaning of Christmas."

26

TURNING POINT OF REVOLUTIONARY WAR

The turning point of the Revolutionary War, the Battle at Trenton, took place in 1776.

1. Investigate and report on this famous battle. Include in your report the names of generals on both sides and the outcome of this famous battle. Indicate in your paper why this battle was the turning point of the war.

PERCOLATER PATENTED

A patent was given to James Nason for his invention, the coffee percolater, in 1865.

1. Coffee is a popular drink in this country. Investigate and report on this crop. Include in your report principal regions where coffee is grown, how it is harvested and processed, and different ways of making the brew.
2. Prepare a large map indicating areas of the world where coffee is grown and harvested. You may either trace or freehand draw the map.

RECORD SNOWFALL

In 1947 the northeastern part of the U.S. had a record snowfall of 26 inches.

1. If you have ever encountered a "record snowfall" in your particular area, write a short account of your experiences. Title your paper "Snowbound."
2. Investigate snowfall records for your area, if you live in a region which annually gets snow. Prepare in chart or graph form U.S. Weather Bureau statistics on snowfall by month, year, or region.

THREE MOST ADMIRED MEN

In 1963 the Gallup Poll stated that the three most admired men in the country were President Johnson, first; former President Eisenhower, second; and Winston Churchill, third. The three most admired women were Mrs. Kennedy, first; Mrs. Johnson, second; and Queen Elizabeth II, third.

1. Write a paper entitled, "The Three Men (or Women) I Admire the Most." State reasons for your choices.

LARGEST INDOOR THEATER OPENS

In 1932 the largest indoor theater, Radio City Music Hall, was opened in New York City.

1. Today the number of movie theaters is on the decline because of their main competition—television. Pretend you have been appointed manager of advertising for the theater

owners. It is your job to prepare a magazine ad which will try to persuade people to attend the movies rather than watching them on television. Use any medium you wish.

2. Write a serious essay entitled, "We Can Do Without Movie Theaters (or Without Television)." State reasons for your opinion.

U.S. OWNS MORE THAN HALF OF ALL TELEPHONES

In 1962 the American Telephone and Telegraph Company reported that the U.S. has 52% of all telephones in the world and for every 100 persons in the U.S. there were 41.8 telephones.

1. Inquire of your local telephone company what the current statistics are for each of the following:
   a. How many people in your town own one telephone?
   b. How many people have more than one phone?
   c. Has the number of phones increased or decreased?
   d. By how many from year to year?
   Illustrate the information you obtain in chart or graph form. Provide a short written summary explanation to accompany your chart or graph.

CONGRATULATIONS, IOWA

The 29th state, Iowa, was admitted into the Union in 1846.
   (Same as #1 and #2 for Nevada, p. 63)

HAPPY BIRTHDAY, PRESIDENT WILSON

President Woodrow Wilson, the 28th President of the U.S., was born in 1856.

1. Investigate and report on the life and contributions of this president.

PLEDGE OF ALLEGIANCE RECOGNIZED

In 1945 Congress officially recognized the Pledge of Allegiance to our flag.

1. Copy this pledge in your best handwriting. Study it and explain in your own words its meaning to you. Also include with your paper the rules for displaying our country's flag.

29

PEPPER POT SAVES THE DAY!

In 1777 an army chef helped prevent mutiny at Valley Forge by devising a new dish, Valley Pepper Pot, a combination of tripe, pepper corns, and vegetables. This dish helped warm the cold soldiers and boosted their morale.

1. Investigate and report on the culinary origins of your favorite foods or dishes. If possible, include both an old and a modern-day recipe for the same dish and contrast the ingredients and methods of preparation.

HAPPY BIRTHDAY PRESIDENT JOHNSON

In 1808 the 17th President, Andrew Johnson was born.

1. Investigate and report on the life and contributions of this president.

CONGRATULATIONS, TEXAS

Texas, the 28th state, was admitted into the Union in 1845.
(Same as #1 and #2 for Nevada, p. 63)

30

GADSDEN PURCHASE

The U.S. acquired from Mexico 45,000 square miles of land known as the Gadsden Purchase, in 1853.

1. Investigate and report on this famous purchase of land. Include in your report a map showing the land acquired.
2. James Gadsden, the U.S. minister to Mexico, was responsible for negotiating this purchase. Investigate and report on the life and contributions of this man.

AUTOMOBILE WORKERS SIT DOWN

In 1936 members of the United Automobile Workers Union had a "sit-down" strike in one of the General Motors Plants in Flint, Michigan.

1. Investigate and report on things which a labor union can do to protect its workers. Include in your paper an explanation of these terms: union, strike, collective bargaining, slow down, closed shop, open shop. Also point out the advantages and disadvantages of belonging to a union. You may wish to interview one or more union members to get their views on the subject.

31

NEW YEAR'S EVE

The approaching new year which begins on January 1 is for many people an occasion for celebration.

1. Investigate and report on the New Year's Eve customs of this country and/or other countries of your choice.
2. The beginning of a new year has traditionally been the time for men to start their lives over again by changing their ways. Traditionally, people make New Year's Resolutions stating how they will improve or change their lives in the coming new year. Prepare your own list of resolutions. Title your paper, "I Resolve." Try to make your resolutions realistic.
3. Prepare a bulletin board or poster display of important news events which occurred during the past year. You may wish to present the material in news reel fashion through a series of pictures with captions and brief comments, or create your own drawings of important events.
4. January 1 is New Year's Day and December 31 is New Year's Eve according to the calendar we follow. However, this was not always the case. Investigate and report on the different calendars that have been used throughout history.

December Game of the Month
Vocabulary Maze

Players: 2, 3, or 4
Grade level: elementary
Materials: One game board (see diagram page 109), 1 die or cube of wood marked same as die; 4 markers of different colors

(use buttons, bottle caps, disks cut from construction paper, erasers, corks, spools, poker chips, etc.); deck of 50 to 100 3 x 5 cards on which vocabulary words from one discipline have been written on one side and the meaning on the reverse side.

Note: Teachers may wish to devise several sets of vocabulary card decks based on different disciplines. Also include in each deck four cards marked "insurance markers."

Rules
1. Students decide by a convenient method who will go first.
2. All players' markers begin on the "start" square.
3. The first player throws the die and advances his marker the number of squares shown on the die. If the player lands on a "bonus" square he does not need to draw from the card deck but takes the bonus indicated on the square. If the player lands on a "penalty" square, he must either do what is indicated on the penalty square or, if he has previously drawn an insurance marker, he may return this marker card to the deck's bottom and not accept the penalty. If the player lands on a blank square, he must draw from the card deck, and read aloud the word and state its meaning. The card is then turned over for verification. If the player gives a correct answer, his marker can remain on the square where it landed and the next player takes his turn. If the player gives the wrong answer, he must return his marker to the square where he was before taking his turn. If desired, players may decide to "play rough" which means when a player gives a wrong answer he must return all the way back to the "start" square.
4. The winner is the first player to reach the "winner" square. Players who are close to the "winner" square must throw on the die the exact number of squares required to reach the winning square. If the player does not do this, he must skip his turn and try on the next turn.

Variation:
1. Play the same as directed above but call it History Maze and use historical facts instead of vocabulary words.

DIRECTIONS FOR CONSTRUCTING VOCABULARY MAZE GAME

The diagram for the Vocabulary Maze game appears on page 109. The length of the maze will vary according to the size of poster-

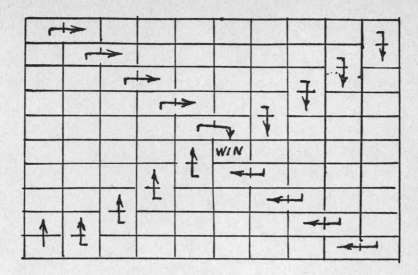

board used; each square should be approximately two inches. For lower grade levels, it is recommended that the maze be relatively simple, while upper grades with longer attention spans might welcome the challenge of a more complex maze.

After constructing the diagram for the maze, indicate routes by arrows. The majority of squares should be left blank indicating to the player that he must draw a card from the card deck. Devise a few bonus squares which allow the player to advance on the game board without having to answer a question such as, Move Ahead three spaces, Take Another Turn, Take Two More Turns, etc. Also devise a few penalty squares which do not allow the player to advance on the gameboard such as, Go Back Three Spaces, Go Back to Start, Skip a Turn, Draw Two Cards, etc.

Chapter Five

January

SLAVES FREED

In 1863 President Lincoln freed the slaves by signing the Emancipation Proclamation.
1. Secure a copy of this famous document and read it. State the main points in your own words. Include in your paper the significance of this famous proclamation and a brief list of events leading up to the proclamation.

HOMESTEADERS STAKE CLAIMS

In 1863 the Homestead Act went into effect. The first homesteader was Daniel Freeman, who staked a claim near Beatrice, Nebraska.
1. Investigate and report on the provisions of this famous land act and indicate in your report its significance.

TOURNAMENT OF ROSES

The first Tournament of Roses was held in Pasadena, California in 1886.
1. Investigate and report on the history of this famous tournament/parade. You may wish to write the Chamber of Commerce in Pasadena to secure information for your report.

2. Construct your own miniature version of a float for the Tournament of Roses. Use a small cardboard box as the base. Construct figures, symbols, and decorations which are appropriate to the current year's theme for the parade. Although the real floats must be entirely made from flowers, you need not adhere to this ruling in constructing your miniature float, but try to incorporate some flowers (either real, artificial, or in picture form) into your float's theme. You may wish to write to the Chamber of Commerce in Pasadena, California to determine the current year's theme.

2

FIRST FLAG OF CONTINENTAL ARMY

In 1776 General Washington flew the first flag of the Continental Army.
1. Investigate and report on this flag. Include in your report a physical description of the flag, as well as a picture or drawing showing its design. Trace the development of the American flag from this period in history to the present time. Try to include pictures or drawings of some of the early flags of ur country.
2. Pretend you have been commissioned by the Continental Army to create several designs for a Continental Army Flag for submission to General Washington for approval. Use any medium you wish and create several designs. Prepare also a brief explanation of the significance of each symbol and color used in your designs.

FIRST WHITE HOUSE SECRETARY

In 1890 the first woman to be employed in the Executive Office of the U. S. President, Miss Alice Sanger, began her job as secretary.
1. If you are interested in the job of secretary as a possible future career, investigate and report on this occupation's training, education requirements, starting salary, benefits, advantages, disadvantages, projected future demand, etc. If possible, interview someone who is presently working as a

secretary to find out what duties are involved in the job. Write a report summarizing your findings.

3

"MARCH OF DIMES" ORGANIZED

The "March of Dimes" campaign was organized in 1938 to collect money to fight polio.

1. Today polio is no longer the dread disease it once was thanks to polio vaccinations. Investigate and report on the discovery and use of the polio vaccine and its significance in helping eliminate this disease.

CONGRATULATIONS, ALASKA

In 1959 Alaska was admitted into the Union as the 49th state.
(Same as #1 and #2 for Nevada, p. 63)

4

CONGRATULATIONS, UTAH

The 45th state, Utah, was admitted into the Union in 1896.
(Same as #1 and #2 for Nevada, p. 63)

5

FIRST WOMAN GOVERNOR

The first woman to be sworn in as Governor of a state, Mrs. Nellie Taylor Ross, took her office in the state of Wyoming, in 1925.

1. Investigate and report on the topic "Women in Politics."

HEART OF WINTER

In those parts of the country which experience seasonal changes, the month of January may often be the coldest, cruelest, and in some ways the most beautiful. It is sometimes called the "heart of winter."

1. If you like winter, compose a poem entitled "The Joys of Winter"

2. Prepare a winter mural entitled "January," showing activities in which people in your area participate during this month.
3. Investigate and report on winter statistics which are of interest to you such as temperature, amount of snow or rainfall, number of accidents related to the weather, sales of winter-related products, etc. Summarize your information in the form of a chart or graph. Accompany each chart or graph with an explanation of the major points presented.
4. Consult an anthology and read several poems about the month of January or winter. Using a medium of your choice, illustrate one or more of these poems. Include with your illustration a copy of the poem in your best handwriting.

6

TELEGRAPH DEMONSTRATED

In 1838 Samuel Morse and his partner demonstrated publicly for the first time their invention, the telegraph.
1. Prepare for display a visual presentation of the Morse Code.

HAPPY BIRTHDAY, MR. SANDBURG

Poet, writer, and Lincoln biographer Carl Sandburg was born in 1878.
1. Investigate and report on the life and contributions of this writer.
2. Read one of Sandburg's poems or a short selection from his biography and using any medium you wish, illustrate one or more scenes.

CONGRATULATIONS, NEW MEXICO

In 1912 the 47th state, New Mexico, was admitted into the Union.
(Same as #1 and #2 for Nevada, p. 63)

"FOUR FREEDOMS"

In 1941 President Franklin Roosevelt made his famous "Four Freedoms State of the Union" speech in which he called for freedom of speech, freedom of worship, freedom from want, and freedom from fear

1. Write a short essay either explaining Roosevelt's Four Freedoms or explaining your own four freedoms and their importance to you.

HAPPY BIRTHDAY, PRESIDENT FILLMORE

The 13th president, Millard Fillmore, was born in 1800.
1. Investigate and report on the life and contributions of this president.

RAILROAD MADE UP OF HORSES?

A carriage drawn by horses over a stretch of track was the beginning of commercial railroad service started by the Baltimore and Ohio Railroad Company in 1830.
1. Investigate and report on the history of railroading in this country. If possible, include pictures of past, present, and future railroad cars.

FANNIE FARMER WRITES BEST SELLER

In 1896 Fannie Farmer published her first cookbook which was a best seller.
1. Make your own collection of recipes and compile into booklet form. Your recipe booklet should have a central theme such as: recipes which young children can make; recipes of famous people; recipes handed down generation to generation; recipes for fast, convenience foods; recipes which use a central ingredient; or recipes for one type of commodity such as candy, cookies, cakes, etc. If you desire, you may wish to illustrate some of your recipes, and of course you will want to make an attractive, eye-catching cover for the booklet. Be sure all recipes are copied in your best handwriting, give exact measurements and directions, and indicate yield. If desired, compute the cost per serving also.

FIRST BOAT THROUGH CANAL

In 1914 the first self-propelled boat made its way through the Panama Canal, although the canal was not officially opened until August 15.

1. Investigate and report on the history of this famous canal. Also include in your report a map showing its location and explain the significance of such a canal.

BATTLE OF NEW ORLEANS

In 1815 General Andrew Jackson successfully defeated the British in the Battle of New Orleans and became a national hero.
1. This famous battle took place two weeks after a treaty had been signed ending the War of 1812, but communication in those times was poor. Write a paper contrasting present-day communication with communication as it was in 1815. What do we have now that they did not have then? How was news received back in 1815?
2. Investigate and report on the life and contributions of this famous general and president.
3. Investigate and report on the major events of the War of 1812. Explain in your paper the reasons for the war and what was gained or lost by each side.

MARIGOLD PROPOSED AS NATIONAL POSY

In 1965 a Senator from Illinois, Everett Dirksen, proposed that Congress make the marigold the national flower of the U. S.
1. If you were asked to present to Congress your ideas on a national flower, what would you recommend? Prepare a statement explaining your choice and reasons for that particular choice. Include with your paper at least one picture showing the national flower of your choice.

FIRST BALLOON FLIGHT

In 1793 the first successful balloon flight was accomplished by Jean Pierre Blanchard in Philadelphia.
1. Investigate and report on the topic "Modern-Day Use of Balloons."
2. Make a balloon flight part of the main plot of a short story you compose in which you are one of the main characters.

FAILURE TO RAISE FLAG CAUSES RIOTS

In 1964 anti-American demonstrations broke out in the Panama Canal Zone because students attending the Zone's high school did not raise the flag of Panama along with the flag of the U. S.
1. Investigate and report on the country of Panama.
2. Investigate and report on the construction of the Panama Canal and its significance to modern-day shipping.

COMMON SENSE

In 1776 Thomas Paine published his pamphlet called *Common Sense* which stated reasons for separation of the colonies from England.
1. Investigate and report on the life and contributions of this separatist.

FIRST GENERAL ASSEMBLY MEETS

The first session of the General Assembly of the United Nations took place in 1946 when people representing 51 nations met in London.
1. Investigate and report on the history of the United Nations, its organization, functions, and present location of its headquarters.

HAPPY BIRTHDAY, MR. HAMILTON

Alexander Hamilton was born in 1757.
1. Investigate and report on the life and contributions of this famous statesman.
2. Mr. Hamilton was the first Secretary of the Treasury. Write a report explaining the functions and organization of the Treasury Department.

CIGARETTE SMOKING HAZARDOUS TO HEALTH

In 1964 the Surgeon General of the U. S., Luther Terry, released a report explaining that cigarette smoking was a hazard to health and might result in lung disease.

1. Using any medium you wish, create a poster or bulletin board display entitled "Don't Smoke." You may wish to contact the local chapter of the American Cancer Society for literature on the subject.
2. Investigate and report on the effects of smoking and its relationship to lung disease and other diseases. You may wish to contact the local chapter of the American Cancer Society or heart and lung associations for literature on the subject.

LASALLE BEGINS LAST EXPLORATION

In 1687 Rene Robert Cavelier, Sieur de LaSalle, began his last exploration on the coast of Texas.
1. Investigate and report on the life and contributions of this explorer.

HAPPY BIRTHDAY, MR. HANCOCK

John Hancock, famous American patriot and statesman, was born in 1737.
1. Investigate and report on the life and contributions of this patriot.

"VICTORY SAUSAGES"

Because of a shortage of meat during World War II, it was announced in 1943 that frankfurters would be replaced by "victory sausages" which would contain some meat and meat substitutes.
1. Find out if "victory sausages" are still with us today. Investigate several different brands of hot dog packages in your local supermarket and list the ingredients of each. Try to determine what percentage of the hot dog is really meat and what percentage is meat substitutes. Consult consumer magazines for additional information on the hot dog and meat substitute story. Summarize your conclusions in a written report.

13

GEORGIA FOUNDED

In 1733 James Oglethorpe along with 130 other colonists established a settlement in what is now the state of Georgia.
  1. Investigate and report on the life and contributions of this colonist.

WELL-KNOWN COMPOSER DIES PENNILESS

Stephen Foster, a well-known composer, died in 1864 a penniless man.
  1. Make a Stephen Foster Medley tape; instrumental, vocal, or both, containing excerpts or complete selections of Foster's music. If you are musically talented, you may wish to tape your own performance.
  2. Investigate and report on the life and contributions of this composer.

TOM SAWYER BAD FOR CHILDREN

In 1877 a literary critic of the *New York Times* said Mark Twain's book, *The Adventures of Tom Sawyer*, was too sinister for children to read.
  1. Read this famous story and report on your reading in a form your teacher suggests. Include in your report an explanation of why a critic might not want children to read the story.

FIRST RADIO WORKS UP TO ONE MILE

In 1906 the Electro Importing Company in New York advertised the first radio set which was supposed to work up to one mile and sold for $7.50.
  1. Investigate and report on the history of radio.

14

ASSEMBLY LINE INTRODUCED

In 1914 Henry Ford introduced the assembly line method of manufacturing automobiles.

1. Investigate and report on the life and contributions of this famous manufacturer.
2. Investigate and report on assembly line production of cars. You might wish to write the Public Relations Department of Ford Motor Company or another car manufacturer for information.

DONKEY REPRESENTS DEMOCRATIC PARTY

In 1870 a political cartoon appeared in *Harper's Weekly* symbolizing the Democratic Party as a donkey.
1. Make a collection of political cartoons. Mount each cartoon on a sheet of paper and explain in your own words what the cartoon is saying.
2. Try your hand at drawing a cartoon which states your viewpoint on an issue involving your school or local community.

POEM INSPIRES ARTIST

In 1899 Edwin Markham published his poem, "The Man with the Hoe," in a San Francisco newspaper after being inspired by Millet's painting with the same name.
1. See if you can be inspired in the same way. Look through a book collection of famous paintings or visit a local art museum or gallery and write a poem which has the same title as one of the paintings.

PENTAGON COMPLETED

In 1943 the Pentagon Building, headquarters for the U. S. Department of Defense, was completed in Washington, D.C.
1. Investigate and report on the organization and functions of the U. S. Department of Defense.

CIVIL SERVICE STARTS
The Pendleton Act which created the Civil Service Commission went into effect in 1883.

    1. Investigate and report on the Civil Service Commission and the types of jobs which are available.

"NOBLE EXPERIMENT" BEGINS

In 1920 prohibition started with the passage of the 18th amendment.
1. Investigate and report on the period in our country's history from the temperance movement to the repeal of the 18th amendment.
2. Using any medium you wish, create a poster or bulletin board display entitled the "Effects of Alcohol."

WILLIE MAYS SIGNS BIG CONTRACT

Baseball player Willie Mays signed a contract for $105,000 making him the highest paid baseball player during the 1965 season.
1. Investigate and report on the life and contributions of this famous baseball player or another famous baseball star, living or dead. Include in your report your views on whether or not baseball players and other sports stars should receive such high salaries. Give reasons for your position.

HAPPY BIRTHDAY, MR. FRANKLIN

Benjamin Franklin, the famous American inventor, author of *Poor Richard's Almanac*, and statesman, was born in 1706.
1. Investigate and report on the life and contributions of this statesman.

DENMARK SELLS VIRGIN ISLANDS

In 1917 the U. S. purchased the Virgin Islands from Denmark.
1. Investigate and report on this U. S. possession. Include in your report the location, principal cities, capital city, population, major industries, climate, and location.
2. Free-hand draw or trace a large map showing the Virgin Islands. Indicate on the map, capital and principal cities, major waterways and mountains, if any, and other points of interest.

QUIZ SHOWS ARE DISHONEST

In 1962 during the "quiz show scandals" ten contestants who had appeared on television quiz programs admitted being given questions and answers in advance.

1. Using a committee of "volunteers," create your own version of a popular television quiz show. Give your performance before your classmates but keep your show honest.
2. Do you believe in the old saying, "Honesty is the best policy?" Write an essay on the topic of honesty. Are there any times when it is alright for a person to be a little dishonest? Is everyone completely honest?

18

HAPPY BIRTHDAY, MR. WEBSTER

The famous orator and statesman, Daniel Webster, was born in 1782.

1. Investigate and report on the life and contributions of this statesman.

SCOTT FINDS HE'S SECOND

In 1912 the English explorer, Robert F. Scott, reached the South Pole only to find that the Norwegian explorer, Roald Amundsen, had reached the same point five weeks earlier.

1. Investigate and report on the life and contributions of both of these modern-day explorers.
2. Investigate and report on the continent in which the South Pole is located.

19

HAPPY BIRTHDAY, MR. LEE

Robert E. Lee, Commander-in-Chief of the Confederate Army during the Civil War, was born in 1807.

1. Investigate and report on the life and contributions of this general.

HAPPY BIRTHDAY, MR. POE

The famous American poet and writer, Edgar Allen Poe, was born in 1809.

1. Investigate and report on the life and contributions of this writer.
2. Read one or more of Poe's stories. Write a short report on your reading in a format your teacher suggests.
3. Using any medium you wish, illustrate a portion of Poe's poetry or one of his stories.

HONOR SYSTEM VIOLATED

In 1965 the U. S. Air Force Academy announced there was an investigation of a violation of the honor system. It was alleged that some cadets had been cheating. Two months later an official explanation said some of the cadets had stolen exam questions.

1. If you saw one of your classmates cheating during an examination, would you tell the instructor? Write a paper explaining your thinking on this question. Give reasons for your views. Indicate whether you feel cheating is alright in some situations.

PRESIDENT SWORN IN

Every four years the President of the U.S. is sworn into office on this day.

1. If the present year is an inauguration year, read the newspapers and/or news magazines to learn of the planned activities and write a summary of the events related to the president's inauguration.

FIRST BASKETBALL GAME PLAYED

In 1892 the first game of basketball was played in Springfield, Massachusetts at the International Y.M.C.A. Training School.

1. Investigate and report on the history of this indoor sport or another indoor sport of your choice. Include in your paper the sport's origins, factors which have increased or decreased the sport's popularity at present, and the outlook for the sport's future. Also include an explanation of why this is your favorite sport.

ROOSEVELT BEGINS FOURTH TERM

President Franklin Roosevelt was inducted into a record fourth term in the office of U.S. President in 1945.

    1. Investigate and report on the life and contributions of this man who served our country for so many terms of office.

HAPPY BIRTHDAY, MR. JACKSON

Confederate General Thomas Jackson, popularly known as "Stonewall," was born in 1824.

    1. Investigate and report on the life and contributions of this famous general.

FIRST ATOMIC SUB LAUNCHED

In 1954 the Nautilus, the first atomic-powered submarine, was launched.

    1. Investigate and report on the history of the submarine. Also include in your report the expectations for submarine usage in the future.

HAPPY BIRTHDAY, LORD BYRON

In 1788 the English poet, Lord Byron, was born.

    1. Investigate and report on the life and contributions of this poet.

    2. Read some of Lord Byron's works. Using any medium you wish, prepare an illustration of one or more of his works.

FIRST AMERICAN NOVEL PUBLISHED

The first American novel written by Mrs. Sarah Wentworth Morton was published in 1789.

    1. Prepare a book report on the best American novel you have read. Use a format suggested by your teacher.

    2. Survey at least 20 adults to determine which American novel is their favorite. Prepare a report and chart summarizing the results of your survey.

3. Using any medium you wish, prepare a book jacket for your favorite American novel. The jacket should have an attractive picture representing the story on the cover, and on the inside flaps a brief biography of the author. The back of the jacket should contain quotations from critics (or from friends and classmates who have read the book and found it enjoyable).

EGGS AND ROSEMARY RECOMMENDED AS SHAMPOO

In 1906 readers of *The Ladies Home Journal* were told that the right shampoo for dark hair was a pint of hot rain water, one ounce of spirits of rosemary, and the yolk of an egg.

1. Using any medium you wish, create a bulletin board or poster display entitled, "How to Take Care of Your Hair."
2. Read in consumer magazines to determine which shampoo is the best and report on your findings.
3. Make a price comparison of shampoos sold in your area by various kinds of stores (drug, discount, supermarket, etc.). Prepare a chart of your findings and a written summary indicating which stores sell a particular brand of shampoo at the lowest price. Be sure to compare shampoos which have equal volume.
4. Survey your friends and/or classmates to find out which shampoo they think is best. Write a report summarizing the results of your survey. Try to find out what "special" or "extra" ingredients your friends use, such as lemon, egg, rain water, beer, etc.

DUMMY GETS $10,000

In 1937 a news story in *Literary Digest* reported that the ventriloquist, Edgar Bergen, set up a trust fund in the amount of $10,000 for continuous care and maintenance of his dummy, Charlie McCarthy.

1. Perhaps you are an amateur ventriloquist. You do not need a fancy "dummy" to perform. Use a simple doll or stuffed toy or hand puppet. Give a demonstration of your talents before your classmates.

24

GOLD RUSH STARTS

In 1848 the discovery of gold by James Marshall, who was building a sawmill for John Sutter, started the famous gold rush of 1848-49.
1. Investigate this famous "gold rush" period of our country's history and report on your findings. Include in your paper the starting and ending dates for the gold rush, the significance of this period in our country's history, the contributions or disruptions of the gold seekers, and why gold was so valuable and is still valued today.

BOY SCOUTS ORGANIZED

In 1908 Sir Robert Baden Powell organized the first Boy Scout troop in England.
1. Investigate and report on the history of the Boy Scout movement. If you are presently a Cub or Boy Scout, include in your paper an explanation of your troop's activities, its objectives, past and present activities, and contributions made to society.

"ESKIMO PIE" PATENTED

Christian Nelson, creator of the "Eskimo Pie" (ice cream brick enclosed in a coating of chocolate) received a patent for his invention in 1922.
1. Investigate and report on the topic of patents.
2. Perhaps you or someone you know have created ice cream inventions worthy of patents. If so, make a recipe collection of these ice cream creations. Copy each in your best handwriting giving exact ingredients and directions. Be sure to give the "inventor" credit for his invention. If you wish, illustrate these inventions using any medium you wish. Also indicate for each recipe cost per serving, and yield.

ATOMIC ENERGY COMMISSION CREATED

The United Nations Atomic Energy Commission was organized in 1946.

1. Investigate and report on the history, functions, and organization of this Commission. You may wish to write to the U.N. to secure information for your report.

SHAY'S REBELLION STARTS

On this day in 1787 a revolt known as Shay's Rebellion took place.
1. Investigate and report on this rebellion. Include in your paper the leader, number of men involved, the significance of this event, and the reasons behind the rebellion.

CROSS-COUNTRY TELEPHONE DEMONSTRATED

In 1915 for the first time telephone service across the U.S. was demonstrated when Alexander Bell in New York City talked to his assistant in San Francisco.
1. Investigate and report on the life and contributions of this famous inventor.
2. Today conversations between people living on the east and west coast are commonplace. Investigate and explain in writing, or picture form on a poster, what the American public can expect of telephone service in the future. You may wish to contact your local telephone company for information and/or pictures for your report.

BEN FRANKLIN ENDORSES TURKEY

In 1784 Ben Franklin wrote a letter to his daughter in which he stated he felt the eagle should not be the national bird of the U.S. He wished to substitute the turkey in its place.
1. Many others since Franklin's time have voiced some disenchantment with the eagle as our national bird. What do you think? Is there another bird that you think better represents this country or should it remain the eagle? Write a paper explaining your views on the subject. Be sure to state reasons for your viewpoint. If you believe another bird should be given this honor, include a picture or drawing of the bird of your choice.

CONGRATULATIONS, MICHIGAN

Michigan, the 26th state, joined the Union in 1837.
  (Same as #1 and #2 for Nevada, p. 63)

AMERICANS ASKED TO GO WHEATLESS AND MEATLESS

Americans were asked in 1918 to stop eating things made of wheat on Mondays and Wednesdays, of meat on Tuesdays, and of pork on Thursdays and Saturdays to help save meat and grain.

1. Pretend that you are the editor of a food magazine and have been asked to develop one week's menu for a family of four which will meet the above qualifications for meatless and wheatless eating. Make sure that all menus are economical and practical to prepare. Compute the cost of each ingredient and cost per serving based on current prices. Be sure that the week's meals provide all the essential servings from the four basic food groups.

NATIONAL GEOGRAPHIC SOCIETY ORGANIZED

The National Geographic Society was started in 1888 in Washington, D.C.

1. Investigate and report on this society's functions, organization, and contributions to society. You may wish to write to them for information for your report.

U.S. WITHDRAWS FROM CUBA

In 1909 the U.S. withdrew for the second time from Cuba.

1. Investigate and report on the U.S.'s first and second withdrawal from Cuba. State the reasons for both occasions.

U.S. COAST GUARD ORGANIZED

The U.S. Coast Guard was officially created by Congress in 1915.

1. If you are interested in serving in the Coast Guard or another military agency as a possible career, investigate the military branch of your choice to determine qualifications for

entrance, education and training programs available, salary, benefits, advantages, disadvantages, etc. Report on your findings.

2. Investigate and report on the history of the Coast Guard. You may wish to write to this agency to secure information for your report.

NO MORE 10 CENT CUP OF COFFEE

In 1954 the increasing price of coffee made American restaurants change the price of a cup of coffee from 10 to 15 cents; inflation caused a pound of coffee to sell for $1.35 in grocery stores.

1. Investigate and report on the current price of coffee and explain what factors affect the price such as inflation, crop failures, supply and demand, etc.
2. Using any medium you wish prepare a large map showing the major coffee growing regions of the world.

HAPPY BIRTHDAY, PRESIDENT McKINLEY

In 1843 the 25th President, William McKinley, was born.

1. Investigate and report on the life and contributions of this president.

"THE RAVEN" PUBLISHED

Edgar Allan Poe's poem, "The Raven," was first published in 1845 in the *New York Evening Mirror*.

1. Read this and other poems and stories written by Mr. Poe. Explain in your own words the meaning of each poem.

CARNATION DAY

The Carnation League was organized in 1903 and requested that every January 29 be known as Carnation Day since this day is the anniversary of President McKinley's birth and the carnation was his favorite flower.

1. If you have a favorite flower, assume you have been requested to form a league, like the Carnation League, whose objective will be to help popularize the flower. Explain in writing the name of your flower league, the day of the year

you would declare in honor of that flower and why you selected that particular day. Explain ways in which people might be encouraged to wear or use your favorite flower.

CONGRATULATIONS, KANSAS

In 1861 the 34th state, Kansas, entered the Union.
(Same as #1 and #2 for Nevada, p. 63)

HAWAIIAN QUEEN PROCLAIMED

Hawaii proclaimed as Queen, Liluiokalani, in 1891.
1. Investigate and report on the history of Hawaii's royalty.
2. Using any medium you wish, free-hand draw or trace a large map of Hawaii. Indicate on the map all the islands which comprise this state, major cities, capital city, and other major points of interest.
3. Investigate and report on the state of Hawaii. Include in your report a brief history, major industries, major cities, capital city, population, climate, and other points of interest.

"HALL OF FAME" ELECTION

The first five men to be elected to the Baseball Hall of Fame were named in 1936. These men were Ty Cobb, Walter Johnson, Christy Mathewson, Babe Ruth, and Honus Wagner.
1. Investigate and report on the life and contributions of one or more of these five famous baseball players.

LIBRARY OF CONGRESS REBUILT

In 1815 the Library of Congress was restored after it had been burned by the British the previous year.
1. If you were given the responsibility of creating a new library for your school or home, and assuming you had limited funds and could not buy more than 25 books, which books would you recommend buying? Write a paper explaining your choices and reasons for these selections.
2. Explore your local or school library to determine exactly what is available and report on your findings.

THE FIRST LONE RANGER

The "Lone Ranger," a national radio favorite, was first broadcast in 1933.

1. If you listen to the radio regularly, write a paper entitled, "My Top Ten Radio Shows." Explain in your paper why you like each show, what time the program is broadcast, its duration, and the station which carries it.

2. Obtain a radio script (or write one of your own or use a play from a book) and by yourself or with the help of volunteers tape a short radio program for your classmates to hear. Remember to include sound effects and your own commercials.

3. The "Lone Ranger" was one of many heros of the west. Investigate and report on the topic, "Heros of the West, Real and Imagined."

31

LEE MADE COMMANDER

In 1865 the President of the Confederacy, Jefferson Davis, appointed Robert E. Lee commander-in-chief of the Confederate Army.

1. Investigate and report on the life and contributions of one or both of these Confederate leaders.

HYDROGEN BOMB DEVELOPED

In 1950 President Truman announced that he ordered the development of the hydrogen bomb.

1. Investigate and report on the history of the atomic age. Include in your report an explanation of the differences between the atom and hydrogen bomb and the uses to which atomic energy has been put in the past and can be put in the future.

EXPLORER I LAUNCHED

In 1958 the first earth satellite of the U.S., Explorer I, was launched; in 1961 a chimpanzee named Ham was sent into space in a Mercury capsule on this same day.

1. Investigate and report on the history of the U.S. Space Program. Include in your report projects for future space flights.

January Game of the Month
Multiplication Derby

Players: 2, 3, or 4
Grade Level: elementary
Supplies: One poster board showing Derby (see diagram on page 132); four small plastic, metal, or clay toy horses, or pictures or drawings of horses pasted on wooden pegs (ads in magazines or children's coloring books are good sources for pictures of horses); one deck of 50 to 100 3 x 5 cards containing multiplication problems on one side and answers on the other; pencils, scratch paper or "Magic Slates."

Rules:
1. Each player will select a horse as his marker. All horses are placed in the "start" gate on the game board.
2. When ready to start, a card is drawn from the card deck. This card is placed on the table in clear view of all players. Each player copies down the problem on his scratch paper and tries to solve the problem as fast and as accurately as he can. Problems must be copied in legible form and all computations must be shown on the paper. No player may confer with another on the solution of a problem, and each player should shield his work from view of others.
3. When a player thinks he has accurately solved the problem, he turns over the card to verify his answer. If his answer is correct, he advances his horse one square on the game board and selects the next card from the deck which he places second in line after the first card drawn in plain view of all players. He must now begin working on the second card's problem. If his answer is not correct, he must continue working the problem until he can get the correct answer. If a player is completely stumped and cannot solve the problem, he may announce "pass" and move his horse backward to the starting gate before continuing on the next card's problem.

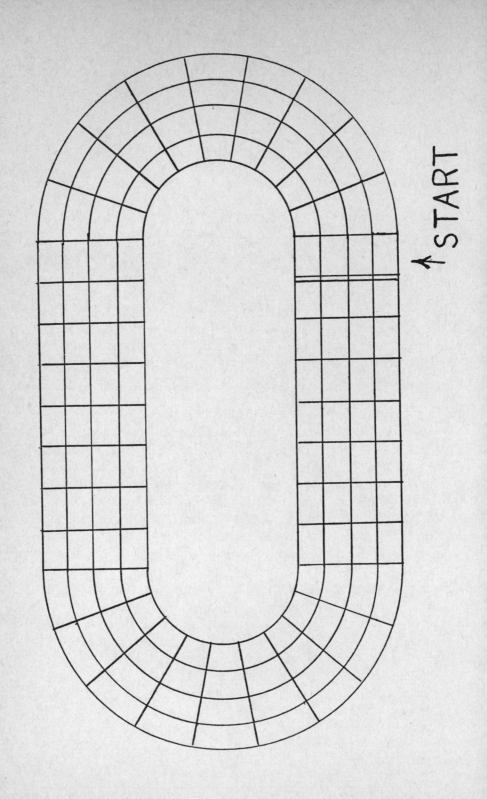

START

4. The winner is the first horse to complete the track once and return to the starting gate.

Variations

1. Play as above but depending upon the ability level of the class, increase the difficulty of the problems by using multiplication problems which involve several digits, decimals, percentages, fractions, etc.
2. Play as above but include in card deck other mathematical computation problems besides multiplication.

Chapter Six

February

1

FIRST SUPREME COURT MEETING

The Supreme Court of the U.S. held its first meeting in 1790 in New York City.

 1. Read that portion of the Constitution which explains the organization and functioning of the Supreme Court of the U.S. Prepare a report explaining the functions, and organization of this highest court in the land.

"BATTLE HYMM OF THE REPUBLIC"

In 1862 Julia Howe, disliking the words Union troops were singing to the song "John Brown's Body," wrote new words entitled "Battle Hymm of the Republic."

 1. Perhaps there is a song which has a melody you like but you do not like the words. Write your own words to an existing melody and submit a copy of the lyrics you composed.

2

GROUND HOG DAY

This day is known as Ground Hog Day. According to the legend, if the ground hog or woodchuck sees his shadow, there will be another 6 weeks of winter; if he does not see his shadow, spring will soon be coming.

1. Investigate and report on other legends, myths, or customs related to predicting the weather, such as the thickness of fur on animals, the depth of fish in lakes, etc.
2. Investigate and report on present-day methods of predicting the weather.
3. Keep track of the weatherman's weather predictions for a period of several weeks. Use the same source each day (either radio, television, or newspaper) and check on the accuracy of prediction of temperature, general atmospheric conditions, rain/snowfall amounts etc. Write a report explaining how accurate the predictions were and include data in chart or graph form to support your paper.

NATIONAL BASEBALL LEAGUE ORGANIZED

In 1876 the National Baseball League was organized when 8 teams banded together.
1. Investigate and report on the history of the National Baseball League. Include in your paper the present teams which comprise this league and their standing for the current or last season.

HAPPY BIRTHDAY, MR. GREELEY

Horace Greeley, a famous American journalist, was born in 1811.
1. Investigate and report on the life and contributions of this journalist.

AMERICAN HEART MONTH

The entire month of February is known as American Heart Month.
1. Prepare a poster or bulletin board display entitled "Be Kind to Your Heart," showing ways in which you can take care of your heart through proper health.

CONFEDERATE STATES OF AMERICA FORMED

In 1861 delegates from 6 states formed the Confederate States of America.

1. Investigate and report on the history of the Confederate States of America. Be sure to include in your report a list of the states which belonged to this organization.
2. Speculate on how it might have been if the Confederacy had won the Civil War and write your views on this subject.

YELLOW FEVER HITS CUBA

In 1901 Major William Gorgas of the U.S. Army began a fight to eliminate yellow fever in Cuba.
1. Investigate and report on this disease and its present-day treatment.

MANKIND NUMBERS IN BILLIONS

In 1962 it was estimated by the Population Reference Bureau that 77,000,000,000 persons have lived on earth since the beginning of mankind.
1. Prepare a chart showing the populations of different countries of the world as they presently stand and the estimated total present population of the world.

TYPICAL BREAKFAST INCLUDES SPRATS, BEER, AND WINE

In 1762 a typical English breakfast for well-to-do people was reported by the Earl of Colchester to be two pieces of salted fish, half a dozen red herrings, a dish of sprats, a quart of beer, and a quart of wine.
1. Today's breakfast tastes have changed and there are many people who skip breakfast. Using any medium of your choice, prepare a poster or bulletin board display entitled, "Breakfast—The Most Important Meal of the Day." Your display should encourage breakfast skippers to eat this important meal.
2. Survey all your classmates and teacher to determine how many skip breakfast and what kinds of foods they eat for breakfast on any given day. Prepare a report summarizing your findings and a chart to illustrate the data you collect.

HAPPY BIRTHDAY, MR. BURR

Aaron Burr, a famous statesman, was born in 1756.

1. Investigate and report on the life and contributions of this statesman.

"LAME DUCK" BECOMES EFFECTIVE

In 1933 the 20th or "Lame Duck" Amendment went into effect.

1. Read and explain in your own words the meaning of this amendment. Explain why the amendment has this unusual name.

CASTRO SHUTS OFF WATER

In 1964 Fidel Castro, leader of Cuba, ordered the water shut off to the U.S. Naval Base at Guantanamo Bay in reprisal for four Cuban fishing boats being seized in U.S. waters.

1. Investigate and report on our neighbor, Cuba. Include in your report the major industries, principal cities, capital city, population, present form of government, and a brief history of the country.

HAPPY BIRTHDAY, MR. DICKENS

In 1812 the famous English writer Charles Dickens was born.

1. Investigate and report on the life and contributions of this famous writer.
2. Read one or more of Mr. Dicken's stories or novels, or a portion of a novel. If you read just a portion, illustrate a scene from your reading using any medium you choose. If you read the entire novel or story, report on your reading in a format suggested by your teacher.
3. Many of Mr. Dicken's stories have been made into movies. If possible, read a novel which has been made into a film and write a paper contrasting the movie with the book. Was the movie faithful to the book? Which story did you like better

and why? Were the characters the way you had pictured them when reading the book?

HAPPY BIRTHDAY, MR. LEWIS

Another famous writer and the first American to win the Nobel Prize for Literature, Sinclair Lewis, was born in 1885.
(Same as #1 and #2, p. 137)

VICE PRESIDENT GETS FLAG

President Roosevelt ordered the creation of a flag for the office of Vice President of the U.S. in 1936.
1. Using any medium you wish, create a design suitable for the Vice President's flag. Be prepared to explain the significance of the colors and symbols your design contains.

HAPPY BIRTHDAY, MR. SHERMAN

William Sherman, a Union general famous for his "march to the sea," was born in 1820.
1. Investigate and report on the life and contributions of this general.

BOY SCOUTS OF AMERICA ORGANIZED

In 1910 the Boy Scouts of America were founded by William Boyce.
1. Write a history of scouting in this country. Include your projections for scouting in the future.

HAPPY BIRTHDAY, PRESIDENT HARRISON

The 9th President, William Harrison, was born in 1773.
1. Investigate and report on the life and contributions of this president.

CONFEDERATE ELECTIONS

Jefferson Davis was elected President of the Confederacy and Alexander Stephens Vice President in 1861.

1. Investigate and report on the life and contributions of one or both of these Confederate leaders.
2. Write a paper on the history of the Confederate States of America. If you wish, instead of writing, submit a pictorial history using pictures and/or drawings to illustrate the history of this short lived organization.

SPANISH PIRATE HONORED

In 1904 Tampa, Florida began holding a Gasparilla Carnival in honor for Jose Gasparilla, a Spanish pirate.

1. Read a novel or story about pirates and report on your reading in a format your teacher suggests.

DEATH OF A SALESMAN

Death of a Salesman, voted by the New York Drama Critics the Best American Play of 1948-49, opened in New York.

1. Read a play and report on your reading in a format your teacher suggests.
2. Try writing your own play called Death of a rule (you fill in the blank). If possible, get "volunteers" to perform your play before the class.
3. If possible, view a live performance of a play, either amateur or professional, and write your own critical evaluation. What did you like and dislike? Would you recommend it to others? Why?

"GERRYMANDER" INTRODUCED

In 1812 the word "gerrymander" was introduced into the English language.

1. Investigate and report on the history behind the word "ger-rymander." Include in your report an explanation of how the word is used in politics today.

YALTA AGREEMENTS SIGNED

In 1945 the Yalta Agreements were signed by President Roosevelt representing the U.S., Winston Churchill representing Great Britain, and Marshall Stalin representing Russia.
1. Investigate and report on the life and contributions of one or more of these famous national leaders.

GEORGIA DAY

This day is known as Georgia Day in the State of Georgia and is set aside to commemorate the day in 1733 when James Oglethorpe landed in Savannah.
1. Investigate and report on the life and contributions of this colonist.

HAPPY BIRTHDAY, PRESIDENT LINCOLN

In 1809 the 16th President, Abraham Lincoln, was born.
1. Investigate and report on the life and contributions of this president.

HAPPY BIRTHDAY, MR. DARWIN

Also born on this day in 1809 was the famous British scientist, Charles Darwin, who developed the theory of evolution.
1. Investigate and report on the life and contributions of this scientist.
2. Explain in your own words the theory of evolution developed by Darwin.

FIRST U.S. MAGAZINE PUBLISHED

In 1741 the first magazine to be published in the U.S., *The American Magazine or a Monthly View of the Political State of the British Colonies,* was issued by Andrew Bradford. This was followed three days later by Ben Franklin's magazine, *The General Magazine and Historical Chronicle.*

1. Which magazines do you read? Why? Prepare a report explaining which magazines you read regularly, which features of these magazines you like and dislike and why. Also include recommendations for your friends as to which magazines they should read and why.
2. Survey your classmates and/or adults to find out which magazines they read regularly. Include at least 20 people in your survey. Write a report summarizing your findings. Include a chart with your report showing data collected. Try to classify the magazines into groups such as news, teenage, fashion, food, decorating, gardening, hobby, etc.
3. Pretend you have been assigned the task of producing an editorial which will appear in the first or second magazine to be issued in the U.S. Compose a short editorial stating your opinion and trying to persuade others to your way of thinking about an issue which would have been of major concern to the people living during that period of history.

"BLUE DANUBE WALTZ"

In 1867 Johann Strauss conducted the famous Blue Danube Waltz for the first time in Vienna, Austria.

1. Prepare a tape containing excerpts of your favorite Strauss music for your classmates to hear.
2. Investigate and report on the life and contributions of this famous composer.

POLE VAULT RECORD

In 1959 a new world record in indoor pole vaulting was established by Don Bragg when he cleared the pole at 15 feet 9½ inches.

1. Investigate and report on the topic, World Records in Sports. Choose one or more sports of interest to you and find the current world records held by various athletes. Briefly mention the training required to attain these world records.

HAPPY VALENTINE'S DAY

This day is Valentine's Day.

1. Investigate and report on the customs and legends associated with the celebration of this day.

CONGRATULATIONS, OREGON

In 1859 the 33rd state, Oregon, was admitted into the Union.
(Same as #1 and #2 for Nevada, p. 63)

CITRUS INDUSTRY BEGINS

In 1886 the citrus industry of the West Coast began when a trainload
of oranges left Los Angeles bound for the East.
   1. Pretent you are in charge of advertising for the West Coast
      Citrus Growers. Use any medium you choose and prepare a
      magazine ad or billboard sign which advertises the merits of
      western-grown citrus fruits. Try to stress the nutritional
      values.

CONGRATULATIONS, ARIZONA

The 48th state, Arizona, was admitted to the Union in 1912.
(Same as #1 and #2 for Nevada, p. 63)

HAPPY BIRTHDAY, GALILEI

In 1564 the famous astronomer and mathematician, Galileo Galilei,
was born.
   1. Investigate and report on the life and contributions of this
      scientist.

MAINE BLOWN UP!

In 1898 in Havana Harbor the U.S. battleship, Maine, was
destroyed; this action lead to the declaration of war with Spain in
April.
   1. Investigate and report on the history of this war with Spain.

NO SLEEP FOR 276 HOURS

In 1964 a man from Finland, Toivo Silvo, established a world record
for going without sleep when he stayed awake for 276 consecutive
hours.
   1. Investigate and report on the topic of sleep. Include in your
      paper the cycles of sleep, why some people need more or less
      sleep than others, and the number of hours required by an
      average child and adult.

16

CUBA HAS NEW PREMIER

In 1959 the leader of the Cuban revolution, Fidel Castro, began his job as premier.
1. Investigate and report on this country. Include in your report its present form of government, principal industries, principal cities, capital city, and brief history.
2. Investigate and report on this revolution which changed Cuba's form of government. Try to find out reasons for the revolution and why it was successful.

17

SARDINES CANNED

The first sardine was canned in 1876.
1. Pretend you have been hired by this cannery to promote the sale of sardines and other fish. Using any medium you wish, prepare a magazine or billboard ad advertising the merits of sardines and other fish. You might wish to investigate a nutrition book to determine the food value of fish or survey cooks or cookbooks to obtain tantalizing sardine or fish recipes which you might portray in your ad.
2. If possible, tour a cannery located in your area and report on your experience. Include in your paper how the food was prepared, processed, packaged, and sold. What special precautions must be taken to insure safe and healthy canned goods? What special equipment is used? From what parts of the country is the raw product received? How many different products are canned at this plant? Under what brand labels? To where are the cans distributed?

FIRST MODERN ART EXHIBITION

Modern art was introduced for the first time in the U.S. at an exhibition of contemporary French painting in New York in 1913. Artists represented included Picasso, Matisse, Braque, and DuChamp.
1. Investigate in an art book, museum or gallery examples of "modern art" by these artists and others. Once you have a feeling for "modern art," try your own hand at creating modern art using any medium you wish.

2. Investigate and report on the life and contributions of one or more of the artists mentioned above.

18

JEFFERSON DAVIS TAKES OFFICE

Jefferson Davis, President of the Confederacy, was sworn into office in 1861.
1. Investigate and report on the life and contributions of this southern leader.

NEW PLANET DISCOVERED

The planet, Pluto, was discovered in 1930. The astronomer Clyde Tombaugh is credited with the discovery.
1. Investigate and report on the most distant planet known in our galaxy, Pluto.
2. Find out the size of the 9 planets in our galaxy. Using balloons, balls, or wads of paper to represent the sun and the planets, prepare a model showing the comparative size of each planet in relation to the sun. Try to make your model free-standing by mounting it in some way such as hanging the parts by string from a clothes hanger.
3. Investigate the planets in our galaxy and prepare a posterboard or bulletin board display showing the number of revolutions it takes each planet to make one complete trip around the sun, the distance each planet is from the sun, and whether or nor the possibility of life as we know it exists.

19

HAPPY BIRTHDAY, COPERNICUS

The famous astronomer, Copernicus, was born in 1473.
1. Investigate and report on the life and contributions of this scientist. Compare his work with that of another astronomer, Ptolemy.
2. If you have an interest in any phase of astronomy as a possible career, investigate and report on it. Include in your paper the training and education requirements, beginning salary,

benefits, expected future demand, advantages and disadvantages of the occupation.
3. If you have an interest in any aspect of astronomy, investigate and report on the topic.

PHONOGRAPH PATENTED

In 1878 Thomas Edison was awarded a patent for his invention, the phonograph.
1. Investigate and report on the life and contributions of this inventor.
2. Construct a collage of Mr. Edison's many inventions.

POST OFFICE CREATED

George Washington signed into law the first Postal Act which created the Federal Post Office in 1792.
1. Today the Post Office is known as the U.S. Postal Service. Investigate and report on the history of the postal service in this country.
2. During Washington's time the cost of sending a letter depended upon the distance the letter had to travel to reach its destination. Today a letter can go anywhere in the U.S. for the same price. However, the cost of this service is going up. Interview at least 20 adults to determine their opinions on how efficient the present postal system is, what they think should be done to keep down the increasing cost of postage, and how they feel about recent price increases. Summarize the results of your survey and include a chart which shows how the majority of people responded to your questions.
3. Using any medium you wish, create a design for a stamp which would commemorate the founding of the Federal Post Office.

FIRST AMERICAN IN ORBIT

In 1962 the first American to go into orbit, John Glenn, Jr., circled the earth three times in a space capsule.
1. Investigate and report on the life and contribution of this astronaut

2. The U.S. has come a long way since that day in 1962. Investigate and report on the history of our country's space program and what is planned for the future.

EARTH GETS PICTURES OF MOON

In 1965 the Ranger Eight spacecraft landed on the moon and sent back to earth pictures of the lunar surface.
1. Write a report on the moon. Include in your paper a description of the moon's surface, atmospheric conditions, if any, temperature ranges, proximity to earth, theories about its origins, and a description of its physical features. If possible, include a picture showing the moon's surface.

21

FIRST TELEPHONE DIRECTORY

The first telephone directory was issued in 1878 by the New Haven, Connecticut Telephone Company.
1. Today telephone directories are common place. However, you may want to be the first to issue a special kind of telephone directory which will be of assistance to students new to your school. This directory might contain the names and telephone numbers of (a) students who are willing to be hosts or hostesses and show new students around the school and town, (b) stores where required school supplies can be purchased, (c) students and/or parents who are willing to serve as tutors in various subjects, (d) organizations and clubs to which students can belong, (e) coaches of local athletic teams. Other information which might be helpful to newcomers can be included, such as maps, a list of school rules, names of teachers and administrators, etc. Make your directory as attractive as possible and organize it for easy use.
2. Today some people do not want to bother looking up a number in their telephone directory; instead they prefer to call the information service provided by most phone companies. Such laziness, however, is costly because the telephone companies must pay people to look up numbers for customers who are too lazy to do it themselves. Using any

medium you wish, create a bulletin board or poster display urging people to use their telephone directories more and call information less.

NEW YORKER PUBLISHED

In 1925 a new magazine called *The New Yorker* was first published.
1. Pretend you have been assigned the job of organizing a new magazine to be called *The* __ (Insert the name of your school or town). What features do you think the citizens of your town or students in your school would like in such a magazine? Write a report describing each department or feature you would include and state reasons for each selection. Also suggest story ideas for the first issue, but do not actually write them.

AMERICAN WHEAT GOES TO RUSSIA

In 1964 the first American wheat shipment arrived in Russia.
1. Some people believe that shipping American wheat to Russia is wrong. It creates higher prices for wheat in the U.S., since there is less wheat to sell here. Others believe that selling wheat to Russia is necessary because higher prices in the U.S. give the farmer more money for his wheat. Other people believe the U.S. has a moral obligation to help starving people since we are a land of plenty and usually produce more than we can eat each year. Still others believe Russia is our "cold war" enemy and therefore should not be helped. Poll at least 20 adults to determine their opinion on this issue. Briefly summarize the results of your survey. State your personal opinion on the issue and whether or not you agree with the majority surveyed.

HAPPY BIRTHDAY, PRESIDENT WASHINGTON

Our first president, George Washington, known as the father of our country, was born in 1732.
1. Investigate and report on the life and contributions of this president.

HAPPY BIRTHDAY, MR. LOWELL

In 1819 the American poet, James Lowell, was born.

    1. Consult an anthology and read a selection of Mr. Lowell's poetry. Using any medium you wish, prepare an illustration of one or more scenes from his poetry.

FIRST DIMESTORE OPENED

The first "dime store" was opened by Frank Woolworth in Utica, New York in 1879.

    1. Investigate and report on the life and contributions of this famous businessman.

HAPPY BIRTHDAY, MS. MILLAY

Another American poet, Edna St. Vincent Millay, was also born on this day in 1892.

    1. Investigate and report on the life and contributions of this poet.

TAYLOR DEFEATS SANTA ANNA

In 1847 one of the most famous battles in the war between Mexico and the U.S. was fought when General Zachary Taylor defeated General Santa Anna at Buena Vista, Mexico.

    1. Investigate and report on the history of this war between Mexico and the U.S. Include in your paper leading generals on both sides, reasons for each country engaging in the war, major battles, and outcomes of the war.

FLAG RAISED ON IWO JIMA

On this day in 1945 six members of the Fifth Division of the U.S. Marine Corps who planted an American flag on top of Mt. Suribachi in Iwo Jima were photographed by an Associated Press photographer, Joe Rosenthal, and this picture was to become the most famous photograph of World War II.

    1. If you have done any photography, create a poster or bulletin board display of your "Most Famous Photographs."

2. If you have an interest in any career related to photography, investigate and report on that occupation. Include in your report the occupation's training and educational requirements, benefits, expected salary, projected future demand, advantages, and disadvantages.

"SILENT HOUR" OBSERVED

In 1965 a company in Germany announced that it would observe a "silent hour" in which all incoming and outgoing telephone calls would be stopped for one hour each day to allow people to concentrate on their work.

1. How do you feel about a "silent hour" each day when no one could talk and it would be illegal to play a radio, television, phonograph, tape, etc.? Write a paper explaining your views on the subject. Explain what people could do during the silent hour and which of these activities you would like and dislike.

SUPREME COURT RULES ON ACTS OF CONGRESS

In 1803 Chief Justice John Marshall made a very important decision, perhaps, the most important ever ruled by the Supreme Court. He ruled that the Supreme Court has the power to declare invalid any law of Congress which was, in the opinion of the Court, unconstitutional.

1. Investigate and report on the Judicial branch of our government. Include in your report some of the major decisions which have been made recently by the Supreme Court.

PRESIDENT JOHNSON TO BE IMPEACHED!

In 1868 the House of Representatives resolved to impeach President Johnson; this was the only impeachment proceeding ever started against a U.S. president.

1. Investigate and report on the impeachment process as described in the Constitution and give background information explaining why impeachment action was taken against this particular president.

FIRST CABINET MEETS

In 1793 the first recorded meeting of a president's cabinet took place when heads of different government departments met at President Washington's home.

    1. Investigate and report on the present president's cabinet. Include in your report the names of its members and their duties.

BILLION-DOLLAR CORPORATION STARTED

In 1901 the first billion dollar corporation, U.S. Steel, was organized by J. P. Morgan.

    1. Investigate and report on the life and contributions of this famous businessman.

INCOME TAX STARTS

In 1913 the first Constitutional amendment passed in the 20th century went into effect giving Congress the power to collect taxes based on a person's income.

    1. Using any medium you wish, make a poster or bulletin board pictorial display of all amendments made to the Constitution up to this date.

    2. Investigate and report on the topic of income tax. Include in your paper an explanation of why such a tax is necessary and what benefits citizens derive from the tax.

NEW CRAZE—DANCE MARATHONS

In 1928 a New York paper reported on the latest national craze, dance marathons, which were popular throughout the country. In a marathon people dance day after day until they can no longer go on and the last couple remaining is the winner.

    1. Compose a short story using the idea of a marathon of any kind as the main plot.

26

HAPPY BIRTHDAY, "BUFFALO BILL"

William Cody, known as "Buffalo Bill," was born in 1846. Mr. Cody was known in the West as an Indian scout and fighter.

1. Investigate and report on the life and contributions of this man.

NEW YORK SUBWAY OPENED

In 1870 the first subway line in New York opened.

1. The subway is only one means of transportation. Using any medium you wish, create a bulletin board or poster display of transportation. Try to include examples of transportation of the future as you see it.

GRAND CANYON NATIONAL PARK ESTABLISHED

In 1919 the Grand Canyon National Park was established by Congress.

1. Investigate and report on the history of this world famous natural wonder.
2. If you have visited this scenic wonder and have photographs or pictures to share with others, mount a display with accompanying explanations, or give a travel talk, presenting the pictures to your classmates with a comment for each picture.

HAPPY BIRTHDAY, MR. LONGFELLOW

On this day in 1807 the poet, Henry Wadsworth Longfellow, was born.

1. Investigate and report on the life and contributions of this poet.
2. Read one or more of Mr. Longfellow's poems. Using any medium you wish, illustrate one or more of his works.
3. Read several of Mr. Longfellow's poems. Try your hand at composing a "take off" on one of his poems. Begin your poem by using one or two of Longfellow's lines but then take off in your own direction. Use the title which Longfellow used.

HAPPY BIRTHDAY, MR. STEINBECK

The American novelist, John Steinbeck, was born in 1902.

1. Investigate and report on the life and contributions of this novelist.

2. Read one of Mr. Steinbeck's short stories or novels and write a report on your reading following the format your teacher suggests.
3. Using any medium you wish, illustrate one or more scenes from Mr. Steinbeck's works.

GERMAN GOVERNMENT SUPPRESSES LIBERTIES

In 1933 the German government under Adolf Hitler issued a proclamation which suppressed civil liberties.
1. Investigate and report on the life of this German leader.
2. Investigate and report on what civil liberties were suppressed by the German government. Comment on how you would feel if these liberties were taken away from you.

LEAP YEAR DAY

This is an extra day which comes once every four years.
1. Investigate and explain why it is necessary to include an extra day in February once every four years. Include in your report an explanation of any customs or traditions which have developed and become associated with Leap Year.
2. Investigate and report on the different calendars which have been used throughout history.
3. Investigate and report on where the names of the days and months originated.

WELL-BRED WOMEN SHUN PERFUME

In 1906 the readers of *The Ladies Home Journal* magazine were told by the editor that well-bred women no longer used perfume.
1. Today the use of perfumes by both men and women is a widely accepted custom and has led to the creation of a large perfume industry. Investigate and report on the history and manufacture of perfumes and also include in your paper an explanation of the difference between perfume, cologne, and toilet water

February Game of the Month
Cross Country Geography

Players: 2, 3, or 4
Grade level: elementary
Materials: One large posterboard map of the U.S. including Alaska and Hawaii, showing state border lines, with each state numbered; a collection of 25-30 markers of the same color for each player (markers could be circles cut from construction paper, or poker chips, buttons, bottle caps, etc.); a deck of 3 x 5 cards with the numbers 1 through 50 on one side and on the other, the name of the state corresponding to that number, the state's capital city, and its neighboring states.

Rules:
1. Players decide by a convenient method who will go first.
2. The first player shuffles the cards and draws a card revealing a number. The player must locate on the gameboard the state which has that number and place one of his markers within the state's boundary lines.
3. Each player scores as follows: 1 point for each state the player can identify, 1 point for naming the state's capital city, one point for naming each state which borders that state.
4. Play continues in this way with each player taking his turn at drawing from the card deck and trying to locate the state on the map. When all cards have been drawn the winner is the player with the most points. Should a player fail to identify a state, he gets no points and his card is placed on the bottom of the deck.

Variations:
   Play as above but use a map of the world. Several posterboards placed side by side may be necessary. Players can identify countries of the world, capitals, neighboring countries. If desired, names of oceans, continents, famous rivers, lakes, seas, mountain ranges, etc. could also be added. Call the game "Around the World."

Chapter Seven

March

1

CONGRATULATIONS, OHIO

In 1803 the 17th state, Ohio, was admitted into the Union.
(Same as #1 and #2 for Nevada, p. 63)

CONGRATULATIONS, NEBRASKA

In 1867 Nebraska was admitted as the 37th state of the Union.
(Same as #1 and #2 for Nevada, p. 63)

YELLOWSTONE NATIONAL PARK CREATED

Yellowstone National Park was created by Congress in 1872.
1. If you have visited this park and have pictures or photographs, make a bulletin board or poster display of your pictures with accompanying written explanations or make an oral presentation to the class in which you share your pictures and memories of your visit. Or, create an imaginary trip.

OLD SAYING ABOUT MARCH

An old saying says that "If March comes in like a lamb it goes out like a lion," and vice versa.
1. Write a paper explaining what this old saying means. Do you think it is true? You may wish to gather statistics from the local weather bureau, radio or television station, and find out! State resources used.

2. Read several poems about March in an anthology. Write a "take-off" on one of the poems read using the first line or two as a starting point, or construct a poem of your own which describes the month of March. You might even like to try writing some Haiku poetry.

PEACE CORPS ESTABLISHED

President Kennedy established the Peace Corps in 1961.
1. Investigate and report on the history of this unique presidential creation. Include in your report an explanation of the purpose of the Corps and how and where it existed. If you know of anyone who served in it, interview them. Ask about their personal reactions to the program, where they served, what they did, etc., and include the interview as part of your report. Would you like to serve? Why?

TEXAS INDEPENDENCE DAY

On this day in 1837 the U.S. recognized the state of Texas as independent from Mexico.
1. Research and write a paper giving the background for Texas' independence being recognized by the U.S. Be sure to state sources used.
2. Assume you are a citizen currently living in the state of Texas. Write a paper describing what life would be like if Texas had not won its independence and you were a citizen of Mexico, not the U.S. You might wish to consult resources to determine Mexico's traditions, customs, and culture.

MT. RAINIER PARK ESTABLISHED

Mt. Rainier National Park was established in 1899. (Same as No. 1 under Yellowstone on p. 154)

TIME BEGINS PUBLICATION

In 1923 a new weekly news magazine called *Time* was first published.
1. Read the current issue of *Time* or another weekly news magazine. Summarize the different features contained in the magazine.

2. Most weekly news magazines contain national and international news. Try writing a small weekly news magazine which contains only local news. You may wish to have the same or similar features and format that the weekly news magazine follows or invent another format of your own. Your news stories should be short and contain news about your school, neighborhood, and town. Design an appropriate cover, and if you wish, include some pages of advertisements.

3. Compare *Time* magazine with other weekly news magazines. How are they different, similar? How do they compare with newspapers?

3

CONGRATULATIONS, FLORIDA

The 27th state, Florida, was admitted to the Union in 1845.
   (Same as #1 and #2 for Nevada, p. 63)

HAPPY BIRTHDAY, MR. BELL

On this day in 1847 the man credited with inventing the telephone was born.

1. Consult a science book or other resource to determine how the telephone works. Make a diagram on posterboard or the chalkboard. Write a short paper, or give an oral presentation to the class using your diagram to explain how the telephone works.

2. Consult the local telephone company to determine their projections for new telephone models and new uses. Bring back pictures or literature describing these projections for the future. Share what you learned with the class through a written paper or an oral presentation.

NATIONAL ANTHEM DECLARED

In 1931 Congress declared "The Star Spangled Banner" as the national anthem of the U.S.

1. Create a poster or bulletin board display of rules to follow when the American flag is displayed or the national anthem played

4

CONGRATULATIONS, VERMONT

The 14th state, Vermont, was admitted to the Union in 1791.
(Same as #1 and #2 for Nevada, p. 63)

FIRST WOMAN IN CONGRESS

In 1917 the first woman to serve in Congress, Jeanette Rankin, took her seat in the House.
1. Report on the topic of "Women in Politics."

5

BOSTON MASSACRE

In 1770 there was a clash between citizens of Boston and British soldiers which aroused the Boston people to demand removal of the soldiers.
1. Consult a history book and determine exactly what happened during the Boston Massacre. Assume you are a newspaper reporter assigned to cover this event. Write a newspaper account. Remember the five W's of news writing. Also, remember to put the most important facts into the first few paragraphs and the least important facts into the last few paragraphs, in case your story is cut down by the editor.

KITE-FLYING WEATHER

During the month of March there is usually some good kite flying weather, thanks to the March winds.
1. Why not construct a kite? Use any materials which are available. You'll be ready on the first windy day to try your hand at flying it. (Note to teacher: If you wish, have everyone in the class construct a kite. Make it a contest with prizes in several categories: best structural design, best or most unusual decoration, best flyer (stays up the longest as evidenced during recess trials), best kit designed by a boy or girl or partners, etc. Get into the swing of things and construct a kite of your own and try flying it with the class.

SAVE YOUR VISION WEEK

The first week of March is usually known as Save Your Vision Week.
1. Create a bulletin board or poster display using any medium you wish showing ways in which you can save your vision through proper use of lighting, and eye safety precautions.

ALAMO DAY

This day is the anniversary of the fall of the Alamo in 1836. The brutality Santa Anna showed at the Alamo aroused Texans to such fury that they went into another battle with Santa Anna crying, "Remember the Alamo."
1. Read in a history book about the Battle of the Alamo. Assume you have been asked to design a commemorative plate by the local historical society depicting this event. The plate should contain an illustration and the inscription, *Remember the Alamo*. You may wish to use pictures in history books as a guide. Use the medium of your choice and a clean 9-inch paper plate.
2. Investigate and report on the life of Davy Crockett and the contributions he made to the Battle of the Alamo.

"GET A HORSE"

Charles Brady King rode his first automobile around the streets of Detroit in 1896. When his "horseless carriage" broke down, a spectator told him to "get a horse." This became a popular cry heard by many automobile owners when their vehicles broke down.
1. Investigate and report on the history of the "Horseless Carriage." Include in your report projections for the future for the automobile industry.

TWENTY-TWO HAMBURGERS IN 25 MINUTES

To win a bet, a man in Chicago, Thomas Garson, ate 22 hamburgers and 2 quarts of ice cream in 25 minutes back in 1938.
1. Using this idea as the main plot, compose a short story. If possible, try to make your story have a surprise ending.

7

HAPPY BIRTHDAY, MR. BURBANK

In 1849 this famous American, responsible for developing many new
varieties of plants, was born.
1. Investigate and report on the life and contributions of this
   scientist.
2. Follow the footsteps of Mr. Burbank and try your hand at
   experimentation with plants. Obtain potting soil, suitable
   containers, and a variety of seeds or already established
   seedlings. Be scientific in your approach. Set up a hypothesis
   and proceed to test it. Remember to have a control group
   and keep accurate records of the results. Here are some
   hypotheses you might test: Plants grow as well in fluorescent
   light as in natural sunlight; Plants grow as well with
   background music (soft, loud, rock, classical) as plants which
   are not exposed to music;Plants grow as well on X-brand fertilizer as plants which have Y-brand fertilizer; Plants which
   have X-watering pattern grow as well as plants which have
   Y-watering pattern. Perhaps you can think of others. Check
   with your teacher before starting your experiment for suggestions on how to conduct your testing. Maintain a daily
   record of your activities and findings. At the end of your experiment, write up a report stating the hypothesis you tested,
   summary of the results, and your conclusions based on the
   experiment.

8

DOG LICENSE STARTS

New York was the first state to require licensing of dogs for the
protection of lost and stray animals in 1894.
1. Write a paper on the training of a dog and the responsibilities
   of a dog's owner.
2. Compose a short story in which a dog license is part of the
   main plot.

AMERICANS EAT 918 POUNDS OF MILK

The Agriculture Department reported that the average American in 1939 ate 62 pounds of beef, 102 pounds of sugar, 177 pounds of flour, 180 pounds of potatoes, and 918 pounds of milk.

1. Investigate and compare the average dietary consumption of an American living today with those of an American living in 1939. Do Americans consume more or less of these commodities? Include in your paper an explanation or possible reasons why consumption of certain foods has increased, decreased, or remained the same. Draw your own conclusions regarding whether Americans today eat better than Americans did in 1939.

FALSE TEETH PATENTED

In 1822 the first patent for artificial teeth was issued to Charles Graham.

1. Many people require artificial teeth because they did not take proper care of their natural teeth. Using any medium you wish, prepare a bulletin board or poster display of pointers on care of teeth.
2. Prepare a large drawing with accompanying explanation of the different kinds of teeth found in children and adults. Explain in your paper these terms: baby teeth, wisdom teeth.
3. Prepare a large diagram showing the structure and naming the parts of the tooth.
4. Investigate and report on the topic of patents.

FIRST SODA FOUNTAIN

The first soda fountain designed by Gustavus Dows, appeared in Lowell, Massachusetts, in 1858.

1. If a soda fountain is one of your favorite places, visit several of them and conduct a survey. Determine the place which has the best soda, sundae, float, ice cream cone, etc., or the place which has the lowest priced items mentioned above. Compile a report entitled, "Soda Fountain Lover's Guide to the Best (or Cheapest) Goodies," which lists the results of your survey. Be sure to include all soda fountain outlets in your area

by name. If you wish, you might provide a brief description of each place, indicating whether the outlet has carry-out facilities, seating capacity, friendly clerks, quality ice cream.
2. Some people feel that the best soda fountain creations are those made at home. If you feel this way, prepare a "Soda Fountain Home Creation Guide" in which you include recipes for soda-fountain-like desserts gathered from magazines, cookbooks, or people you know. Each recipe should give clear instructions, exact ingredients, yield, and cost per serving. If you wish, you may include an illustration or drawing of some of the recipes, or treat your classmates or teacher to one of the "creations."

BATTLE OF MONITOR AND MERRIMAC

In 1862 the two iron warships, Monitor and Merrimac, battled for four hours off the Virginia coast.
1. Using any medium you wish, prepare an illustration and brief description of this naval battle which took place during the Civil War.

DANIEL BOONE EXPLORES WEST

In 1775 frontiersman Daniel Boone was hired to cut a road through the wilderness.
1. Investigate and report on the life and contributions of this frontiersman.

FIRST PAPER MONEY ISSUED

In 1862 the first paper money was issued by the U.S. in denominations of $5, $10, $20, $50, $100, $500, and $1,000.
1. Investigate and report on the manufacture and issuing of money, both paper and coin, by the U.S. government. Include in your paper an explanation of what happens to old money, where paper money is printed, and how to tell counterfeit money from the real thing.
2. Pretend you have been assigned the task of designing a new $1 paper bill. Using any medium you wish, create several designs which would be appropriate for a new issue of the U.S. $1 bill

3. If you have a paper money collection, prepare a display with accompanying short written explanations, or show your money to the class with an oral description.

11

"BLIZZARD OF 88" BEGINS

On this day in 1888 the famous "Blizzard of 88" began. It dumped a heavy snowfall on the eastern part of the U.S., particularly New York City, where hundreds of thousands of people were marooned in their homes and places of business until the storm subsided 3 days later.

1. If you have ever experienced a real blizzard,write an account of your experiences. Include in your paper a description of what you and the people with you did, and your feelings at that time.
2. Compose a short story using the "Great Blizzard of __" (insert year) as your title and main plot.
3. Investigate and report on the topic of snow. Include in your report an explanation of how snow is created, its advantages and disadvantages, how it differs from ice, which regions of the world get the most and least amount of snow, and other facts of interest.
4. If there is snow where you live, create a snow sculpture.
5. Investigate statistics related to snowfall in your area and represent your findings in graph or chart form. Try to find out one or more of the following: Average snowfall for different areas of the country, different countries, or different parts of your state; Total monthly snowfall for your area, state, or region of the country; Total yearly snowfall accumulation for your region or state.

12

DUKE OF YORK GETS LAND

In 1664 King Charles II of England granted land in the New World, now New Jersey, to his brother, the Duke of York.

1. Investigate and report on the founding of New Jersey.

FIRST PARACHUTE JUMP

The first parachute jump was made by Captain Albert Berry in 1912.
　　1. Investigate and report on the history of the parachute. Include some information about the sport of parachute jumping.

GIRL SCOUTS FOUNDED

The Girl Scouts of America were organized by Mrs. Juliette Lowe in 1912.
　　(Same as #1, for Boy Scouts, p. 125)

HAPPY BIRTHDAY, MR. PRIESTLEY

The discoverer of oxygen, Joseph Priestley, was born in 1733.
　　1. Investigate and report on the life and contributions of this scientist.

"UNCLE SAM" CREATED

In 1852 the first cartoon symbolizing the U.S. government as "Uncle Sam" appeared in the *New York Lantern.*
　　1. Draw your own "Uncle Sam" cartoon or another cartoon using a different symbol. Your cartoon(s) should indicate an idea of political significance.

EVOLUTION NOT LEGAL

In 1925 the Govenor of Tennessee made it illegal for any teacher to teach Darwin's theory of evolution.
　　1. Investigate and report on this theory.

COTTON GIN PATENTED

Eli Whitney patented his invention, the cotton gin, in 1794.
　　1. Investigate and report on the life and contributions of this inventor. What was the cotton gin, and why was it a significant invention?

2. Today fabrics made from natural fibers coexist with man-made fabrics. Investigate and report on the topic "Man-made Fabrics." Include in your report an explanation of how the man-made materials are made and compare their advantages and disadvantages with such natural fibers as cotton and linen.

WAR BONDS ISSUED

The U.S. government issued the first war bonds in 1812. These were issued to help purchase more military equipment for the War of 1812.
1. Investigate and report on the history of this short war between the U.S. and England.

HAPPY BIRTHDAY, MR. EINSTEIN

World-famous scientist, Albert Einstein, was born in 1879.
1. Investigate and report on the life and contributions of this famous man.

HAPPY BIRTHDAY, PRESIDENT JACKSON

The 7th president, Andrew Jackson, was born in 1767.
1. Investigate and report on the life and contributions of this president.

CONGRATULATIONS, MAINE

The 23rd state, Maine, was admitted into the Union in 1820.
(Same as #1 and #2 for Nevada, p. 63)

FIRST OPEN PRESIDENTIAL PRESS CONFERENCE

For the first time in history a president, Mr. Wilson, held an open presidential press conference in 1913.
1. Watch on television or listen on the radio or read in the newspaper about the president's latest press conference. Explain and summarize the major issues and questions covered in this conference and the president's position on these points.

HAPPY BIRTHDAY, PRESIDENT MADISON

The fourth president, James Madison, was born in 1751.
1. Investigate and report on the life and contributions of this president.

MILITARY ACADEMY ESTABLISHED

The U.S. Military Academy at West Point was established by Congress in 1802.
1. If you have an interest in going to West Point or any other military academy, investigate and report on it. Include in your report admission requirements, costs, location, benefits, advantages, and disadvantages.

THE SCARLET LETTER

Nathaniel Hawthorne's book, *The Scarlet Letter,* was published in 1850.
1. Investigate and report on the life and contributions of this writer.
2. Read this novel or another novel or story written by Mr. Hawthorne. Report on your reading in a format your teacher suggests.
3. Using any medium you wish, illustrate one or more scenes from one of Mr. Hawthorne's works.

ST. PATRICK'S DAY

This is St. Patrick's Day, a day set aside to honor the patron saint of Ireland.
1. Investigate and report on the life of St. Patrick and the legends and traditions relating to him.
2. Green is the color commonly associated with the celebration of this day. Compose a story in which the color green is of great importance.

FIRST PRACTICAL SUBMARINE

The first practical submarine in history, created by John Holland, was able to stay submerged for 1¾ hours in 1898.

    1. Investigate and report on the history of submarines.

CAMP FIRE GIRLS FOUNDED

Mrs. Luther Gulick founded the Camp Fire Girls, an organization for young girls, in 1912.

    (Same as #1, for Boy Scouts, p. 125)

HAPPY BIRTHDAY, PRESIDENT CLEVELAND

The 22nd and 24th president of the U.S., Grover Cleveland, was born in 1837.

    1. Investigate and report on the life and contributions of this president.

"BUTTER BOXES" BECOME NECESSITY

In 1923 people in Berlin who ate in restaurants were forced to carry "butter boxes" which contained their own supply of butter because the restaurants refused to provide it due to its high cost.

    1. Use the concept of a ___box (butter or something else) as the main plot of a story you compose.

BIG SALE ON ALARM CLOCKS

In 1944 people jammed a Chicago department store when it was announced that 1,500 alarm clocks, which had been difficult to get since World War II began, would be available.

    1. Think about what it would be like to live in a world where there was no time. Write an essay explaining how no clocks and no concept of time would affect your daily life.

    2. Write a short story using the concept of no time as the main idea.

HUGHES BUYS STUDIO

In 1954 financier Howard Hughes was the first individual to become the sole owner of R.K.O., a major motion picture company.

    1. Investigate and report on the life and contributions of this famous financier.

SWALLOWS RETURN TO CAPISTRANO

On this day the swallows traditionally return to San Juan Capistrano Mission in California.

1. Investigate and report on this phenomenon. How do you explain the birds returning on the same day each year? Are there other occurrences in nature similar to this one? What explanations do scientists have for this?
2. Investigate and report on the topic of "swallows" or any other bird of interest to you. Include in your report a description of the bird, and if possible, one or more pictures; what the bird eats; the kind of nest it makes; how it raises its young; unusual characteristics, if any; general locality where the bird is found; its natural enemies; and other points of interest.

TREATY OF VERSAILLES REJECTED

In 1920 the Treaty of Versailles, which established the League of Nations, was rejected by the Senate.

1. Investigate and report on the League of Nations explaining its organization, function, and reasons why the U.S. did not join.

UNCLE TOM'S CABIN

Harriet Beecher Stowe's book, *Uncle Tom's Cabin*, was first published in 1852 and created a sensation in the book world.

1. Investigate and report on the life and contributions of this writer.
2. Read this famous book and report on your reading using a format your teacher suggests.
3. Using any medium you wish, illustrate one or more scenes from this book.

POLE VAULTING RECORD ESTABLISHED

An indoor pole vaulting record which stood for 16 years was established by Cornelius Warmerdam in 1943 when he vaulted 15 feet 8 1/2 inches.

    1. Investigate and report on world records in sporting events which take place indoors and which are of particular interest to you.

FIRST INDIAN TREATY

The first Indian treaty was made on March 21, 1621 when Governor Carver of the Plymouth Colony pledged friendship and alliance with the Wampanoag Indians.

    1. Investigate and report on significant treaties made with Indians.

FIRST SECRETARY OF STATE

Thomas Jefferson took the office of Secretary of State in 1790 in the cabinet of George Washington.

    1. Investigate and report on the members of George Washington's cabinet. Include brief descriptions of each member and list that member's contribution to history.

ROCKING CHAIR MARATHON

Rocking chair marathons were very popular in Quebec, Canada. In 1955 the champion was Aime' Lavoie who rocked for 81 hours, 3 minutes, 52 seconds.

    1. Try to write as many limericks as you can about any kind of marathon.

    2. Use the rocking chair marathon as the main plot of a short story.

22

STAMP ACT BECOMES EFFECTIVE

In 1765 the much disliked Stamp Act went into effect.

    1. Investigate and report on this unpopular act. Include in your paper the specific items that were taxed; how the law came about; why the colonists did not like it; and what the colonists did about it.

SPRING HAS SPRUNG

In some parts of the country, about this time, people start thinking "spring."
   1. In honor of spring, using any medium you wish, make a bulletin board or poster display of symbols of spring, or construct a spring mural.
   2. Compose a poem about the spring season.
   3. Consult an anthology of poems and read several that have been written about spring. Using any medium you wish, illustrate one or more of these poems.

"GIVE ME LIBERTY OR GIVE ME DEATH"

In 1775 the famous statesman, Patrick Henry, introduced a resolution providing for the organization of an army and in defense of this idea gave his famous "Give me liberty or give me death" speech.
   1. Investigate and report on the life and contributions of this famous statesman.

MELBA TOAST INTRODUCED

In 1901 Opera star, Madame Nellie Melba, described for her fans how she made toast. It soon became known as Melba Toast.
   1. If you have some favorite recipes for making different kinds of toast or dishes which require toast as one of the ingredients, make a collection of these recipes. Include complete directions, exact ingredients and measurements, and yield per recipe. Also, compute cost per serving. If you wish, illustrate one or more of the recipes.

JAPANESE INTERNMENT CAMPS

In 1942 people of Japanese-American heritage living on the Pacific Coast were moved to internment camps inland.
   1. Investigate and report on the internment of the Japanese Americans during World War II. What were the reasons for placing these people in camps? How were they treated? Do you think this was the right thing to do?

SPACE TEAM LAUNCHED INTO ORBIT

In 1965 the first two-man American space team, Virgil Grissom and John Young, was launched into orbit. They became the first spacemen to shift orbits by manual control.

1. Investigate and report on the life and contributions of one or both of these astronauts.

"MY QUEEN" GIVES ADVICE

In 1902 one of the earliest advice columns appeared in a weekly magazine for young women called *My Queen.*

1. If you have a serious problem, write a letter explaining your problem to one or more of the columnists of local news-papers or magazines who give professional advice.

TUBERCULOSIS GERM ISOLATED

Robert Koch announced the discovery of the germ which caused tuberculosis in 1882.

1. Investigate and report on the life and contributions of this scientist.
2. Investigate and report on the disease, tuberculosis. Include in your report a description of the treatment, characteristics of the disease, methods of detection, and prominence of the disease today.

PHILIPPINES GET INDEPENDENCE

The Philippines became independent in 1934.

1. Investigate and report on this country. Include in your paper its principal cities, capital city, major industries, and brief history, and population.
2. Free-hand draw or trace a large map of this country. Show on the map major cities, capital city, and other points of interest.

25

COLONIZATION OF MARYLAND BEGINS

This day marks the anniversary of the landing in 1634 of colonists on St. Clement's Island and the founding of St. Mary's settlement.
  1. Investigate and report on the colonization of Maryland.

FIRST PANCAKES

New Yorkers were amazed as they watched the first public demonstration of making pancakes in 1882.
  1. Make a collection of pancake recipes. Include in your booklet each recipe's exact ingredients, directions, yield, cost per serving, and if you wish, an illustration. You might use as your theme for the recipe booklet the idea of a pancake for each day of the week, and an extra-special one for Sunday.

COAL MINE EXPLODES!

In 1947 a large coal mine explosion occurred in Centralia, Illinois.
  1. Investigate and report on the topic of coal. Include in your report an explanation of how coal is formed; how and where it is mined in this country; working conditions and safety measures taken to protect coal miners.

26

HAPPY BIRTHDAY, COUNT RUMFORD

In 1753 physicist Benjamin Thompson, who became Count Rumford, was born.
  1. Investigate and report on the life and contributions of this physicist.

HAPPY BIRTHDAY, MR. FROST

The celebrated American poet, Robert Frost, was born in 1875.
  1. Investigate and report on the life and contributions of this poet.

2. Read one or more of Mr. Frost's poems and using any medium you wish, illustrate one or more scenes from his works.

ITALY BURNS ITS OWN MONEY!

In 1925 the Government of Italy burned its own money at a public bonfire; this was done to help fight inflation.
1. Investigate and report on the topic of inflation in America. Include in your paper the meaning of the word, inflation, what different people think should be done to fight inflation, and why inflation is good or bad.

LONG DISTANCE CALLING

The first long distance telephone call made between Boston and New York occurred in 1884.
1. Using any medium you wish, prepare a bulletin board or posterboard display illustrating telephone etiquette.

EARTHQUAKE IN ALASKA!

In 1964 one of the worst earthquakes in recent history struck Alaska.
1. Investigate and report on the topic of earthquakes. Include in your paper an explanation of what happens to the earth's crust during a quake, causes of quakes, methods of recording and predicting quakes, and measures which can be taken to prevent loss of life and property during a quake.
2. Investigate and report on the topic "Major Earthquakes in American History."

ENERGY CONSERVATION ENCOURAGED

Even back in 1905 conservation of energy was encouraged. Readers of the current issue of the magazine, *Ladies Home Journal,* were told to make a slow-cooking dish on those days when a steady fire was necessary for the washing and ironing of clothes.
1. Using any medium you wish, create a poster or bulletin board display entitled, "Energy Saving Tips for the Home."

NEW BATHING SUITS

Designers of swimwear predicted in 1921 that ladies soon would be wearing one-piece, form-fitting bathing suits.

1. If you are interested in fashion, either men's or women's, make a collection of drawings and/or pictures which illustrate changes in fashion. Be sure to include time periods for each illustration.

SINGING COMMERCIALS BANNED

In 1944 a New York radio station refused to air singing commercials.

1. Today singing commercials are very popular on both radio and television. Conduct the following survey to find out how well they are remembered by the public. Listen to the radio or television and record at least 10 different singing commercials. Copy the words on a piece of paper using your best handwriting but omit any reference to the product's name. Show these jingles to at least 20 different people. Ask them to read the jingle and identify, if they can, the product associated with it. Write a report summarizing the results of the survey. Draw your own conclusions about the effectiveness of singing commercials.

HAPPY BIRTHDAY, PRESIDENT TYLER

The 10th president of the U.S., John Tyler, was born in 1790.

1. Investigate and report on the life and contributions of this president.

U.S. CAPTURES MEXICAN CITY

In 1847 the city of Vera Cruz, Mexico was captured by General Scott.

1. Investigate and report on the war between the U.S. and Mexico. Include in your paper reasons why the two countries went to war and what was gained and lost as a result.

NEIGHBOR CANADA BECOMES A DOMINION

In 1867 the Dominion of Canada was created by the British Parliament.

1. Investigate and report on America's northern neighbor, Canada. Include in your report a description of the type of

government, resources, principal cities, capital city, provinces and territories, languages spoken, population, size, and other factors of interest. If possible, include with your report pictures showing this country's natural beauty and its people. You may wish to write to the Canadian tourist bureau to secure information for your report.

PENCIL WITH ERASER PATENTED

In 1858 Hyman Lipman received a patent for the first pencil with an eraser.

1. Imagine, if you can, what an inanimate object, such as a pencil, would say if it could talk. How do you think a pencil feels when it is crushed between the pages of a book, or stuffed into a pencil case, or chewed by a nervous student? Use your imagination and write a paper entitled, "Adventures of a Pencil." Write your paper in the first person, singular (I).
2. How many times has an eraser "saved your life?" Can you put your appreciation for the pencil and its companion eraser into poetry? Try. You may want to use the limerick format.
3. Investigate and report on the manufacture of pencils and erasers. Include in your report an explanation of the natural materials required for manufacture and how they are processed. Also, give some thought to what pencils of the future might look like.

SEWARD BUYS ICE-BOX

In 1867 "Seward's Folly" or "Seward's Ice-box," Alaska, was purchased from Russia, much to the disappointment of many people who thought it was a foolish waste of money until gold was discovered there.

(Same as #1 and #2 for Nevada, p. 63)

PARIS GETS TOWER

In 1889 the famous landmark of Paris, France, the Eiffel Tower, officially opened in spite of many protests.

1. Using any medium you wish, create a poster or bulletin

board display of pictures of famous American landmarks.
2. Write a paper entitled "Famous American Landmarks" or "Famous Landmarks of My State." Explain in your paper the reason for each landmark's fame and include a map showing location.

U.S. STARTS DAYLIGHT SAVING TIME

The U.S. began observing daylight saving time for the first time in 1918.
1. The use of daylight saving time has recently been encouraged as a means of energy conservation. Using any medium you wish, create a poster display entitled "Energy Saving Tips."
2. Free-hand draw or trace a large map of the U.S., including Alaska and Hawaii. Indicate on your map the time zones into which the U.S. is divided, and the difference between standard and daylight saving time in each zone.

FIRST BLACK ASTRONAUT

Edward Dwight, Jr., was the first black man to be selected for astronaut training in 1963.
1. Investigate and report on the topic, "Training of Astronauts."
2. Report on the topic, "Famous Blacks in American History."

March Game of the Month
History Rummy

No. of Players: 2, 3, or 4
Grade level: elementary
Materials: Card deck of 3 x 5 cards containing 52 cards in 26 matching pairs of historical terms and/or dates, such as Washington/Father of our Country; December 7, 1941/-Bombing of Pearl Harbor; First 10 Amendments to Constitution/Bill of Rights, etc. Make sure that none of the terms or dates can be used more than once correctly. In the top right-hand corner of each card place the point value. Assign point values to each pair of terms or dates commensurate with difficulty. For ease of computation, point values in variables of 5 are recommended.

Rules:

Play as regular Rummy game as follows—

1. Players decide by convenient method who will deal first. Dealer shuffles cards and deals 7 cards to everyone except the person on his left who gets 8.
2. The player receiving 8 cards discards one card. The player to his left has the choice of selecting the card discarded or drawing a card from the deck. Every player must always discard a card each time he takes a turn.
3. Play continues in this way with each player either drawing from the deck or taking the card previously discarded. As a player finds a match, he places the pair of matching cards on the table in front of him.
4. The winner is the first player to make 3 correct matches. The winner will always have one extra card which he then discards.
5. When a player has made 3 correct matches and the hand has ended, each player is to count up the point values of cards laid on the table and report his score to the scorekeeper. If a player has cards left in his hand, he must deduct the total number of points in his hand from those on the table. If the player has no cards laid out on the table, his score is deducted from the points he earned in previous hands.
6. The winner of the game is the first player to accumulate 150 points.

Variations:

1. Play as above but use vocabulary words from other disciplines.
2. Use the card deck to play Concentration. Players place all 52 cards face down on the table. Each player selects two cards to turn over hoping they will be a match. If the cards match, he removes these cards and earns the points attached to those matching cards. If the cards do not match, he replaces them on the table and the next player takes his turn. Players should remember where cards are located. Players take turns until all cards have been removed from the table. The winner is the one with the most points.
3. Play as directed above but include two "joker" cards which can be played as "wild" cards.

Chapter Eight

April

APRIL FOOL'S DAY

The modern-day custom on this day is to play harmless, practical jokes and tricks upon people.
1. Investigate and report on the origins of April Fool customs.
2. Practical jokes played on other people can be fun but sometimes they are also harmful. Write a short story in which the dangers of harmful practical joking are illustrated.

FIREMEN GET REGULAR SALARY

In 1843 Cincinnati, Ohio was the first city to pay firemen a regular salary, something which other cities were soon to do.
1. If the career of fireman interests you, investigate and report on this occupation. Include in your report the requirements for the job, special training, beginning salary, opportunities for advancement, benefits, advantages, disadvantages, and projected future demand.

WOMAN MAKES BASEBALL TEAM

Virne (Jackie) Mitchell was the first woman in baseball history to be signed up as a regular team member of an otherwise all-male team in 1931.
1. Investigate and report on the topic, "Women in Sports." Include the names of women and their contributions in one or more sports.

2

MINT ESTABLISHED

Congress established a mint to coin money in 1792.
1. Investigate and report on the minting of coins.
2. If you are an American coin collector, display your collection and provide either an oral or written explanation of the value and history of each coin displayed.

HAPPY BIRTHDAY, MR. ANDERSON

Hans Christian Anderson, author of children's fairy tales, was born in 1805.
1. Read one or more of Mr. Anderson's stories and report on your reading in a format your teacher suggests.
2. Write one of your own fairy tales. If possible, read your story to several younger children to see if it holds their interest. If you feel after the "test" that it needs revision, make whatever changes you wish and test it again.

3

HAPPY BIRTHDAY, MR. IRVING

Washington Irving, an American writer, was born in 1783.
1. Read one or more of Mr. Irving's stories and report on your reading in a form your teacher suggests.
2. Investigate and report on the life and contributions of this writer.
3. Using any medium you wish, illustrate one or more scenes from Mr. Irving's stories.

PONY EXPRESS STARTED

The Pony Express was started on this day in 1860.
1. Investigate and report on this unique form of mail delivery.

UNION TROOPS IN CONFEDERATE CAPITAL

In 1865 the capital of the Confederacy was occupied by Union troops.

1. Construct a time line on posterboard showing significant events in the Civil War. If you wish, present your time line from the viewpoint of the North or the South.

CONGRESS WANTS FLAG CHANGED

In 1818 Congress ordered the U. S. flag to be redesigned.
1. Investigate and report on the history of the "Stars and Stripes."
2. Do you think you can come up with a better design for our country's flag than the present one? If so, try your hand at creating a new design. Submit your design in color and explain in writing the significance of each color and symbol used.

VITAMIN C DISCOVERED

In 1932 Professor C. G. King isolated Vitamin C.
1. Using any medium you wish, construct a posterboard or bulletin board display showing food sources of all vitamins.
2. Using any medium you wish, construct a posterboard display of the four basic food groups and indicate the number of daily servings required from each to insure a proper diet of needed nutrients.

VETO PRECEDENT SET

George Washington established a precedent when he vetoed an act of Congress in 1792.
1. Using any medium you wish, create a poster display entitled "How a Law is Born." Be sure to incorporate in your illustration the veto power of the president and the conditions necessary to override a presidential veto.

HAPPY BIRTHDAY, DR. LISTER

The founder of antiseptic surgery, Sir Joseph Lister, was born in 1827.

1. Investigate and report on the life and contributions of this scientist.

GOLD RECALLED

President Roosevelt recalled all gold held by the public in 1933.

1. Throughout history gold has had a tremendous value. Investigate and report on the topic, "Gold." Include in your paper reasons for the value of gold, where gold is found, how it is mined, and present uses for this valuable mineral.

PERRY DISCOVERS NORTH POLE

Robert Perry was the first man to reach the North Pole in 1909.

1. Investigate and report on the life and contributions of this explorer.

U. S. AT WAR WITH GERMANY

The U. S. officially declared war against Germany in 1917, thus marking the beginning of U. S. involvement in World War I.

1. Pretend you were a writer for a news magazine and were assigned the task of writing an article about the U. S. declaration of war against Germany. Start your article out in this way, "Today the U. S. government officially declared war against Germany." Find out what events led to this drastic action and describe them in the following paragraphs.

CLANG, CLANG, CLANG, WENT THE TROLLEY

Trolley cars ran for the last time in New York City in 1957.

1. Using any medium you wish, prepare a posterboard display showing out-moded means of transportation such as the trolley car, Conestoga wagon, Indian canoe, etc.

HAPPY BIRTHDAY, MR. WORDSWORTH

The English poet, William Wordsworth, was born in 1770.

1. Read some of Mr. Wordsworth's poems and using any medium you wish, illustrate one or more scenes.

2. Investigate and report on the life and contributions of this writer.

LONG-DISTANCE TELEVISION

The first successful long-distance demonstration of television took place in 1927 at the Bell Telephone Laboratories in New York.

1. Investigate and report on the history of television and on projections for its use in the future.
2. If you have an interest in a career in broadcasting, investigate and report on that occupation. Include in your paper the job's projected demand, education and training requirements, salary, benefits, advantages, disadvantages, and opportunities for advancement.

EXPLORER SEEKS FOUNTAIN OF YOUTH

In 1513 the Spanish explorer, Ponce de Leon, landed in Florida looking for the Fountain of Youth.

1. Investigate and report on the life and contributions of this explorer.

LEAGUE OF NATIONS ENDS

The last session of the League of Nations took place in Geneva on this day in 1946. The organization adjourned after transferring its powers and assets to the United Nations.

1. Investigate and report on this organization, its founding, its function, and why the U. S. was not a member.

LEE SURRENDERS TO GRANT

Confederate General Robert E. Lee surrendered to General Ulysses S. Grant, Commander of the Union Army in 1865 at Appomattox Court House, Virginia.

1. Investigate and report on the life and contributions of one or both of these famous generals.
2. Construct a time line on posterboard illustrating major events up to and including the Civil War. Present your time line from the viewpoint of either the North or South.

FIRST ASTRONAUTS NAMED

In 1959 the National Aeronautics and Space Administration named America's first astronauts. They were Scott Carpenter, John Glenn, Virgil Grissom, Walter Schirra, Jr., Alan Shepard, Jr., and Donald Slayton.
   1. Investigate and report on the life and contributions of one or more of these men.
   2. Investigate and report on the training of American astronauts.

CHURCHILL HONORARY CITIZEN

In 1963 Sir Winston Churchill was made an honorary citizen of the U. S. by presidential proclamation.
   1. Investigate and report on the life and contributions of this honorary citizen.

SAFETY PIN PATENTED

In 1849 a patent was given to Walter Hunt for his invention, the safety pin.
   1. Compose a short story in which a safety pin is of major significance in the plot.
   2. Write a paper entitled "Where the World Would be Today if it Were Not For Walter Hunt."

SOCIETY FOR ANIMALS

In 1866 the New York state legislature granted a charter to the American Society for the Prevention of Cruelty to Animals.
   1. Using any medium you wish, prepare a bulletin or poster-board display showing pointers pet owners should follow to avoid cruelty to animals.
   2. A recent development in the pet industry is the importing of certain wild animals and selling them as unusual pets. Write a paper about animals which should never become pets and give your reasons why.

11

SPANISH-AMERICAN WAR ENDS

In 1899 the Treaty of Peace was signed with Spain and the Spanish-American war ended.
1. Investigate and report on the history of this war. Include in your paper reasons why each country went to war, events which led up to the declaration of war, and what was gained and lost by both sides as a result of the war.

FIRST BLACK BASEBALL PLAYER

The first black to play on a major baseball team, Jackie Robinson, started with the Brooklyn Dodgers in 1947.
1. Investigate and report on leading black athletes, past and present, in professional sports.

12

CIVIL WAR BEGINS

On this day in 1861 Confederate forces fired upon Ft. Sumter in the harbor of Charleston, South Carolina, thus starting the Civil War.
1. Pretend you were a reporter at the scene of Ft. Sumter. Write a news story about this event keeping in mind the five W's of news writing.

FATHER OF BOMB SUSPENDED

Dr. J. Robert Oppenheimer, known as the "father of the atomic bomb" was suspended from the Atomic Energy Commission in 1954 but later reinstated.
1. Investigate and report on the life and contributions of this scientist.
2. Investigate and report on the Atomic Energy Commission. Include in your report its history, organization and functions.

FIRST HUMAN IN SPACE

In 1961 a Russian pilot, Yuri Gargarin, was the first human to travel in space when he was launched in the space ship Vostok and made a single orbit of the earth in 89.1 minutes.

    1. Russia has long been the biggest competitor of the U. S. in many fields including space. Investigate and report on Russia, our competitor. Include in your report this country's leading cities, capital city, major industries, type of government, population, and other factors which you feel are important.

HAPPY BIRTHDAY, PRESIDENT JEFFERSON

The 3rd president of the U. S., Thomas Jefferson, was born in 1743.

    1. Investigate and report on the life and contributions of this president.

NEW PIANIST DISCOVERED

In 1958 a 23-year old pianist, Van Cliburn, won first prize at the International Piano Contest.

    1. If you are presently studying or have studied this instrument, play either live or on tape for your classmates.

OSCAR AWARDED

In 1964 Sidney Poitier was the first black actor to be awarded an Oscar for a starring role.

    1. Investigate and report on the topic, "Blacks in the Entertainment Field, Past and Present.

FIRST BLACK PAGE

In 1965 the first black page to serve in either house of Congress, Lawrence Bradford, Jr., was appointed.

    1. Investigate and report on the topic of Congressional pages. Include in your paper how one may apply for the job, what duties are involved, age requirement, education required, etc.

FIRST WEBSTER'S DICTIONARY

Noah Webster's first Dictionary was published in 1828.
1. Make your own mini dictionary of specialized words such as spelling words which are difficult for you, science terms, etc. Pattern your mini dictionary after a regular dictionary.

PAN AMERICAN UNION FORMED

At the first Pan American Conference between the U. S. and South American countries in 1889, a resolution was passed forming the Pan American Union. It is composed of republics in North, Central, and South America. The governing board several years later adopted a resolution setting April 14 as Pan American Day, a time to honor all countries in the Union.
1. Select one country, other than the U. S., which is in either North, Central, or South America and investigate and report on it. Include in your report the major cities, capital city, major industries, climate, population, brief history, and other points of interest.
2. Free-hand draw or trace a large map showing all countries in the Pan American Union. Indicate each country's capital city.

HAPPY BIRTHDAY, MR. JAMES

The American writer, Henry James, was born in 1843.
1. Read one of Mr. James' stories and report on your reading in a format your teacher suggests.
2. Investigate and report on the life and contributions of this author.
3. Using any medium you prefer, illustrate a scene from one of his works.

TITANIC SINKS!

In 1912 the luxury liner Titanic struck an iceberg and sank drowning 1,517 people

1. Pretend you were a news reporter on the scene. Prepare a news story about this event. Keep in mind the five W's of news reporting.

INCOME TAX DAY

This is the last day on which an American citizen can pay his income tax without incurring a penalty.

1. Investigate and report on the topic "Income Taxes." Indicate in your report the origin of the income tax and why it is necessary. Explain what this country would do if we had no income tax.

FIRST AMERICAN PLAY

In 1787 the first play written by an American, *The Contrast*, by Royal Tyler, was produced in an American theater.

1. Read an American play which is of interest to you and report on your reading in a format your teacher suggests.
2. Try to write a short play about any theme that interests you. If possible, get "volunteers" from your class to act the play before your classmates.
3. If you have ever attended a live performance of a play, either professional or amateur, and you can still remember this experience, report on the play in a format your teacher suggests.

BRUSSELS WORLD FAIR OPENS

In 1958 the Brussels World Fair opened.

1. If you have been to a world fair, write a report of your experiences. If possible, include pictures or photographs.

BAY OF PIGS INVASION

In 1961 a group of anti-Castro rebels landed in the Bay of Pigs, Cuba and attempted to overthrow the Castro government but failed.

    1. Investigate and report on Cuba's present form of govern-
ment and its leadership under Fidel Castro.

PAUL REVERE'S FAMOUS RIDE

In 1775 Paul Revere made his famous ride to alert people that 800
British soldiers were on their way to Concord where the colonists had
stored their gun powder.
    1. Investigate and report on the life and contributions of this
       patriot.
    2. Read Longfellow's poem about this famous ride and using
       any medium you wish, illustrate one or more scenes from the
       poem.

EARTHQUAKE HITS SAN FRANCISCO!

In 1906 an earthquake which resulted in many fires destroying half of
San Francisco killing almost 500 people, injuring 1,500, and leaving a
quarter million people homeless.
    1. Investigate and report on this famous earthquake. Include in
       your report statistics which explain the damage done and
       how long it took the city to rebuild. Also explain whether
       you would live in a city such as San Francisco which is fre-
       quently hit by earthquakes.
    2. Investigate and report on the topic of earthquakes. Include in
       your report the causes of quakes, parts of the world which
       usually experience quakes, methods of predicting and
       recording quakes, and precautions to take during a quake to
       protect life and property.

LONGEST HOME RUN

In 1953 baseball star, Mickey Mantle, hit a homerun which traveled
565 feet and is presently believed to be the longest measured homerun
in big league history.
    1. Investigate and report on the life and contributions of this
       baseball star.
    2. Investigate and present in graph or chart form baseball
       statistics which are of interest to you.

PATRIOTS' DAY

To commemorate the Battles of Lexington and Concord, which started the Revolutionary War, this day is known as Patriots' Day. In the States of Massachusetts and Maine the anniversary of these battles is a holiday.

1. Investigate and report on these two famous battles and their outcomes.
2. Pretend you were a newspaper reporter assigned the task of covering these famous battles. Write a news story keeping in mind the five W's of the news writing.
3. Pretend that Congress made this day a national holiday and you were assigned the task of creating several different bumper stickers which would remind citizens about Patriots' Day. Use your best printing and any medium you wish.

WAR OF INDEPENDENCE ENDS

It was announced by Congress in 1783 that the Revolutionary War had ended.

1. Construct a poster time line of major events leading up to and including the War for Independence.

U. S. OFF GOLD STANDARD

It was announced in 1933 that the U. S. was going off the gold standard.

1. Investigate and report on the topic, "Gold Standard" and explain the advantages and disadvantages of a country following such a standard. Also include in your report whether our country is presently on this standard.

RADIUM DISCOVERED

In 1902 radium was isolated for the first time by Marie and Pierre Curie.

1. Investigate and report on the life and contributions of one or both of these scientists.
2. Investigate and report on the past and present uses of radium.

21

HAPPY BIRTHDAY, MS. BRONTE

The English novelist, Charlotte Bronte, was born in 1816.
1. Investigate and report on the life and contributions of this writer.
2. Read one of Ms. Bronte's stories and report on your reading in a format your teacher suggests.
3. Using any medium you wish, illustrate one or more scenes from one of Ms. Bronte's works.

$64 DOLLAR QUESTION

The phrase, "$64 question" was used for the first time as part of a radio quiz program, "Take It or Leave it." This phrase referred to the jackpot question which was worth $64.
1. Conduct your own "$64 Question" game. Prepare questions based on subjects your class has studied previously. Arrange the questions into categories and within each category provide both easy and difficult questions which will be valued $4, $8, $16, $32, and the most difficult, $64. Select a master of ceremonies and several contestants, or with your teacher's permission, use the entire class as contestants. Each contestant must select a category and try to answer the questions in the category. If they answer the first question correctly, the receive $4. They then have the option of keeping that $4 or risking it for $8, etc. until they come to the last question, which is worth $64. If the entire class plays, you may wish to have a "play off" between all those who correctly answered the $64 question. Use play money for the prizes or something of real value such as candy, gum, etc. Should any questions arise over a contestant's answer, the teacher will be the judge.

"IN GOD WE TRUST" ADOPTED

In 1864 the U. S. Mint was authorized by Congress to use the motto, "In God We Trust," proposed by a clergyman, Rev. M. R. Watkinson.

    1. Pretend you have been assigned the task of designing a new U. S. coin with a new motto. Using any medium you wish, prepare one or more designs for both sides of the coin. The coin may be of any denomination.

FIRST SHOT BETWEEN AMERICA AND SPAIN

The first shot of the Spanish-American War was fired in 1898.

    1. Investigate and report on the major events leading up to and including this war. Explain what was gained and lost by both sides as a result of this war.

"ROUGH RIDERS" WANTED

In 1898 Theodore Roosevelt began recruiting "rough riders."

    1. Investigate and report on the life and contributions of this president. Include in your paper an explanation of the term "rough riders."

23

HAPPY BIRTHDAY, PRESIDENT BUCHANAN

The 15th president, James Buchanan, was born in 1791.

    1. Investigate and report on the life and contributions of this president.

VOLUNTEERS NEEDED

The government sent out word that 125,000 volunteers would be needed to fight the war against Spain in 1898.

    1. Pretend you were assigned the task of creating advertising posters for this purpose. Using any medium you wish, create several posters asking for volunteers to help fight Spain.

UNFAIR TO CATS

In 1949 the Governor of Illinois, Adlai Stevenson, vetoed a bill requiring cats to be on a leash because he believed this would be unfair to cats.

1. Pretend you were living at that time. Write a letter of either support or argument to the governor. Be sure to state your reasons. Address the letter to Governor Stevenson, care of the Capitol Building, Springfield, Illinois.
2. Most local ordinances require that dogs be on a leash when taken into public; yet cats are not required to be leashed. Do you think this is fair? Do you think this is equal treatment for dogs and cats? What precautions should be taken by dog and cat owners to insure their pet's safety and comfort as well as those of others? Write a paper explaining your views.

FIRST REGULAR NEWSPAPER

The first regularly printed American newspaper, the *Boston News Letter*, was first published in 1704.

1. Publish your own classroom newspaper. You are the editor and it is up to you to decide what types of articles will be included in the paper. You may want to ask some of your classmates for their assistance in producing your first issue.
Think of a good name for your classroom paper and as editor, prepare an editorial on some aspect of school life. Keep in mind the five W's of news reporting when assisting your volunteer "reporters" in writing their news stories.

WHITE HOUSE BURNS!

During the War of 1812 the British burned the Capitol, the White House, and other buildings in Washington, D. C. in 1814.

1. Read about this event in a history book. Pretend you were a reporter from a news magazine sent to cover this story. Write a news story keeping in mind the five W's of news writing and giving some background information about the war to your readers.

TELEVISION FACTS

The 1964 edition of *Television Factbook* reported that there were 143,000,000 television sets in the world and of this number 61,850,000 were in the U. S. At that time 90 nations had television broadcasting and 26 of these banned commercials completely.

1. Determine and publish your own Television Factbook. Interview at least 25 people, children and adults representing 25 different families, to get the answers to these questions about television: How many television sets do you have in your home? On the average, how many hours a day do you and/or your family watch television? What is the favorite children's program in your house? What is the favorite adult program in your house? What things would you like to see changed about television broadcasting? What is your family's favorite television commercial? Would you be willing to pay for television broadcasting if there were no commercials? What channel does your family watch the most? Do you have one or more color sets in your house? If you wish, add other questions to this list. After gathering the answers, tabulate and summarize your results. Present some of your data in the form of graphs or charts.

2. Write a serious essay entitled, "Television, Who Needs It?" Explain in your paper why you feel we should or should not have television and the advantages and disadvantages of watching it.

MEXICAN WAR STARTS

The first shots of the Mexican War were heard in 1846 at La Rosia, Mexico.

1. Construct a poster time line showing major events leading up to and including this war.

AMERICA AT WAR WITH SPAIN

The U. S. Government declared war on Spain in 1898.

1. Prepare a time line depicting important events leading up to and including this war.

NEW YORK STARTS LICENSE PLATES

In 1901 New York became the first state to require license plates on vehicles.

1. Pretend you have been given the task of designing next year's license plates for your state, assuming that each year plates must be changed. Your design should include one or more symbols representing your state, a state motto of your own creation, and colors which are significant to the people and/or history of your state. Submit one or more ideas using any medium you wish.

ST. LAWRENCE SEAWAY OPENED

In 1959 the St. Lawrence Seaway opened.

1. Investigate and report on the benefits derived from this waterway. Include with your report a map illustrating the seaway.

FIRST PERMANENT BRITISH SETTLEMENT

In 1607 the British established their first permanent settlement at Cape Henry, Virginia.

1. Investigate and report on the topic, "Early Settlements in the New World—Their Successes and Failures."

HAPPY BIRTHDAY, MR. AUDUBON

The famous naturalist, John James Audubon, was born in 1785.

1. Investigate and report on the life and contributions of this naturalist.
2. The Audubon Society, named after this naturalist, was organized for the study and protection of birds. If you have an interest in one or more species of birds, prepare a report which includes the bird's physical description, natural habitat, type of food eaten, natural enemies, how the young are raised, and other facts which interest you. If possible, include one or more drawings or pictures of the species upon which you are reporting.

3. Using any medium you wish, prepare a bulletin board or poster display entitled "Birds: What They Do For Us and What We Can Do for Them."
4. Using any medium you wish, prepare a bulletin board or poster display showing birds native to your area.

27

HAPPY BIRTHDAY, PRESIDENT GRANT

The 18th president, Ulysses S. Grant, was born in 1822.
1. Investigate and report on the life and contributions of this president.

U. S. STEEL STARTS GARY

In 1906 the U. S. Steel Corporation started construction of a new town located along Lake Michigan, Indiana, which was to be called Gary.
1. Investigate and report on the history of this town or another town of your chosing, perhaps your own.

"BABE RUTH" DAY

"Babe Ruth" Day was observed by baseball fans in 1947.
1. Investigate and report on the life and contributions of this baseball hero.

28

HAPPY BIRTHDAY, PRESIDENT MONROE

The fifth president, James Monroe, was born in 1758.
1. Investigate and report on the life and contributions of this president.

CONGRATULATIONS, MARYLAND

The 7th state, Maryland, entered the Union in 1788.
(Same as #1 and #2 for Nevada, p. 63)

SIRLOIN STEAK COSTS 24 CENTS POUND

In 1902 the newspaper, *The New York World,* reported on the high cost of living, stating that sirloin steak cost 24 cents a pound, and that lamb chops, pork chops and ham cost 18 cents a pound.

1. Visit a supermarket and note the current prices for these items. Prepare a poster illustrating the contrast in cost of living in 1902 and the present year as measured by the prices of these items. Provide readers of this poster with a means of comparison by showing the average income for a family of four then and now.

TELEPHONE GUARANTEED TO WORK ONE MILE

In 1878 a Boston newspaper carried ads for a $3 telephone guaranteed to work for one mile and a $5 telephone guaranteed to work for five miles.

1. Using any medium you wish, prepare an advertisement for today's telephone and its ability to work for long distances. If you wish, include other aspects of the modern telephone such as touch-tone dialing, speaker-phone, picture-phone, etc. You may wish to contact your local telephone company for information.

ZIPPER PATENTED

The zipper was first patented in 1913.

1. Compose a short paper entitled, "Where Would We Be Without Zippers," or make this gadget an integral part of a short story you compose.

MAH-JONGG CRAZE

The Chinese game, Mah-Jongg, was the craze in almost every state in 1923.

1. Interview at least 30 people, either all adults or all students about your age, to determine what the current craze is in games. Ask each person what game is played most often in his/her house. Tabulate and summarize the results of your survey. Include a chart or graph to represent your data.

2. If you have an idea for a game, try to create it and test it on your classmates. It could be a board game, card game, or game of skill. Submit a written report of your "testing" and a copy or description of the game.

LOUISIANA PURCHASE

In 1803 the U. S. doubled its physical size by buying land from Napoleon Bonaparte for roughly 4 cents an acre; this purchase was known as the Louisiana Purchase and resulted in the addition of 13 states to the U. S.
1. Free-hand draw or trace a large map showing the land purchased from France as part of the Louisiana Purchase. Also indicate the present state boundary lines within this purchase.
2. Investigate and report on the history of this famous purchase. Explain in your report why France sold this territory, how the sale was received by the American people, advantages the U. S. gained from the purchase, and who engineered this purchase for the U. S. government.

CONGRATULATIONS, LOUISIANA

In 1812 Louisiana, the 18th state, was admitted into the Union. (Same as #1 and #2 for Nevada, p. 63)

April Game of the Month
Spelling Baseball

No. of Players: 2 or multiples of 2
Grade level: elementary
Materials: Posterboard showing a baseball diamond; four markers of one color, and four of another (use buttons, bottle caps, corks, poker chips, discs cut from construction paper, etc.); spelling text.

Rules:
1. Each player represents a baseball team and selects four markers of one color to represent his team. Players decide by a convenient method who will go first to bat and who will pitch.
2. The person at bat places one of his markers on homeplate. The team pitching places a marker in the pitcher's box. Play begins with the pitcher pitching a spelling word taken from the spelling text to the batter. The batter responds by spelling the word out loud. There is only one chance to spell the word. If the batter spells the word correctly, he takes first base by placing a marker on it. The pitcher then pitches another word to the batter, or if more than two people are playing, to the next person on the team. If there are more than two players on a team, they must take turns. If the batter correctly spells the second word, the first marker is moved to second base, and another marker is placed on first base indicating two men on base. If a player at bat fails to spell the word correctly or takes too long to determine the spelling, it is considered an "out" for his team. When a team has 3 outs teams change sides.
3. Play continues in this manner through 9 innings. The winning team is the one which scores the most runs.
4. There are no stolen bases or strikes or balls in this version of baseball.

Variation:
For a faster game, make one out, instead of three, the point where sides change.

Chapter Nine

May

1

MAY DAY

The giving of flowers was traditionally done on the first of May.
1. Gather a bouquet of fresh flowers from your garden or an open field or prairie. Place them in water in a decorated container. Follow the May Day custom by placing them on someone's doorstep.
2. Investigate and report on Old and New World customs related to May Day celebrations.

EIGHT-HOUR WORK DAY SET

In 1886 the Federation of Trades meeting set a standard of an 8-hour work day for American labor.
1. Today many economists believe that the 8-hour day will be shortened in the future. Many companies now have people working 37½ or 35 hours a week instead of the customary 40. Shortening the work week means there will be more leisure time and hobbies will become more important. Do you have a hobby? Describe it in writing. Explain how you first got interested in it, the cost involved, the amount of time you spend working on it, the most interesting aspect of your hobby, etc. If possible, bring one or more of your hobbies to school for others to see.

DEWEY DEFEATS SPANISH FLEET

In 1898 Commodore George Dewey defeated the Spanish fleet in Manila Bay.
1. Investigate and report on the life and contributions of this man.

2

REGULAR TELEVISION SCHEDULE APPROVED

The regular scheduling of commercial television programs, to begin on July 1, was approved by the Federal Communications Commission in 1941.
1. Today we take television programs as a source of information and entertainment more or less for granted because we have grown up with the "tube." The variety of programs to which we have become accustomed was not available to early television viewers. If you know of someone who was able to see programs in the early days, interview them to find out what types of programs were available, how often programs were aired, what televisions looked like in the early days, and their reactions to programs that they saw. Ask them to contrast yesterday's programs with today's programming.
2. In most areas of our country today, a wide variety of programs are available from which the viewer can choose. Critics, (people who view programs and comment on them), can help us decide which program to watch. Read several reviews of programs in a television magazine or newspaper. View the programs that have been critiqued and form your own opinions. Write a report summarizing the critics' reactions to each program, and your own. In what cases did you agree? Disagree?
3. Read several critical reviews of television programs to learn the style and format of a critical review. Try to write one or more of your own critical reviews of television programs. State in your paper why you would recommend or not recommend a particular program and why.
4. Write a serious essay entitled, "What Television Needs Today." Explain your views on the subject indicating in your paper the types of programs you would like to see and why.

3

AIRPLANE PASSENGER SERVICE STARTED

In 1919 airplane passenger service was started by Robert Hewitt who flew two passengers from New York City to Atlantic City, New Jersey.
  1. If you have ever flown in an airplane and had an especially delightful flight or a dreadful flight due to poor service or other conditions, compose a letter of commendation or complaint to the airline involved. Send your letter and await your answer. Remember, it is easy to complain, so if you do some complaining, be sure to include constructive suggestions for remedying the situation.

"I AM AN AMERICAN DAY"

In 1940 Congress set the 3rd Sunday of May to be "I Am an American Day."
  1. Write a short paper describing the privileges, liberties, and advantages of being an American.
  2. Create several bumper stickers in honor of this day. Use your best lettering and any medium you wish.

SYNTHETIC QUININE PRODUCED

At Howard University synthetic quinine was produced for the first time in 1944.
  1. Investigate and report on the history of a life-saving or pain-reducing drug such as quinine. Include in your paper the present-day use for the drug, the person(s) who discovered it, and how the drug is manufactured.

4

DUTCH LAND ON MANHATTAN

In 1626 a Dutch colonizer, Peter Minuit, landed on Manhattan.
  1. Investigate and report on the colonization of New York.

HAPPY BIRTHDAY, MR. MANN

Horace Mann, the father of the public school system, was born in 1796.

1. Investigate and report on the life and contributions of this educator.
2. Investigate and report on the history of education in this country. Contrast modern-day schools with those of early colonial days.
3. Write a serious essay entitled "What's Wrong (Or Right) With Our Schools." State your opinions and suggest changes which need to be made. Giving reasons for your thinking.

5

TEACHER ARRESTED FOR TEACHING

In 1925 a biology teacher, John Scopes, was arrested for teaching Darwin's Theory of Evolution which was against state law.

1. Investigate and report on the life and contributions of the scientist, Darwin.
2. Explain in your own words Darwin's Theory of Evolution.

FIRST SPACE EXPLORER

In 1961 Commander Alan B. Shepard, Jr., was the first American space explorer. He was rocketed 115 miles into space and landed 15 minutes later.

1. Investigate and report on the life and contributions of this astronaut.
2. Write a paper explaining the achievements of the American Space Program to date and its outlook for the future.

6

FIRST POSTAGE STAMP ISSUED

In 1840 the first postage stamp in history was issued in England.

1. If you are a stamp collector, bring your collection to school and create a display of your most interesting or prize posses-

sions. Explain in writing or orally interesting facts related to the stamps in your collection.

2. Pretend you have been assigned the task of designing a postage stamp. Using any medium you wish, create a design for a first-class postage stamp. Your stamp may commemorate any important event in this country's social or historical background.

HINDENBURG EXPLODES!

In 1937, as people gathered to watch it, the dirigible, Hindenburg exploded.

1. Investigate and report on the subject, dirigibles. If possible, include with your report a picture or drawing of a dirigible.

HAPPY BIRTHDAY, MR. BRAHMS

The composer Johannes Brahms was born in 1833.

1. Make a tape recording of excerpts of music composed by Brahms for your classmates to hear. Include on your tape a brief commentary about each excerpt.

2. Investigate and report on the life and contributions of this composer.

HAPPY BIRTHDAY, MR. TCHAIKOVSKY

The Russian composer and conductor, Peter Ilich Tchaikovsky, was born in 1840.

1. (Same as 1 and 2 above).

MISSISSIPPI RIVER DISCOVERED

In 1541 Hernando De Soto discovered the Mississippi River.

1. Investigate and report on the life and contributions of this explorer.

FIRST AUTOMOBILE PATENTED

Papers were filed for the first automobile patent in 1879 by George B. Selden.

1. Investigate the history of the automobile and report your findings.

HAPPY BIRTHDAY, PRESIDENT TRUMAN

In 1884 President Harry S. Truman was born.
1. Investigate and report on the life and contributions of this president.

MT. PELEE ERUPTS

A volcanic eruption on Mt. Pelee on the Island of Martinique destroyed the entire town in 1902.
1. Write a paper entitled "Volcanos." Explain in your paper the causes of volcanic eruptions, the names of active volcanos and when they last erupted.
2. Free-hand draw or trace a map of the world and locate on this map major volcanic activity within the last 100 years.

FIRST MEN FLY OVER NORTH POLE

In 1926 the first men flew over the North Pole. They were Commander Richard E. Byrd of the U. S. Navy and Floyd Bennett.
1. Investigate and report on the life and contributions of Mr. Byrd.

NAZIS BURN BOOKS

In 1933 Nazi leaders burned 25,000 books which were considered forbidden reading.
1. How do you feel about a government burning books which it thinks the citizens should not read? Write a report explaining your viewpoints. Give reasons why you think this is good or bad.

COLUMBUS BEGINS LAST VOYAGE

In 1502 Christopher Columbus began his fourth and last voyage.
1. Investigate and report on the life and contributions of this explorer.
2. Free-hand draw or trace a map showing the four voyages of Columbus and his party.

[10]

"GREEN MOUNTAIN BOYS" ATTACK

In 1775 the British fortress at Ticonderoga, New York was attacked by the Green Mountain Boys led by Ethan Allen.
 1. Investigate and report on the life and contributions of Mr. Allen and his famous Green Mountain Boys.

CONFEDERATE PRESIDENT CAPTURED

In 1865 the President of the Confederate States, Jefferson Davis, was captured.
 1. Investigate and report on the life and contributions of this southern leader.

RAILROAD CONNECTS EAST WITH WEST

In 1869 the last golden spike was driven into the railroad which connected the eastern with the western part of the country. The first transcontinental railroad in America was finished.
 1. Investigate and report on the history of railroading in this country. Include in your report prospects for railroads in the future.
 2. Make a bulletin board or poster display of pictures or drawings illustrating various kinds of railroad cars and their uses. If possible, include pictures of railroad cars of past, present, and future.

CONFEDERATE MEMORIAL DAY

This day is a legal holiday in North and South Carolina in honor of the Confederacy.
 1. Using any medium you wish, prepare several bumper stickers in honor of Confederate Memorial Day.

[11]

HAPPY BIRTHDAY, JOHNNY APPLESEED

Johnny Appleseed, whose real name was John Chapman, was born in 1768.
 1. Investigate and report on the life and contributions of this folk hero

2. Read a story about Johnny Appleseed or some other figure in American folk lore and report on your reading in a format your teacher suggests.
3. Using any medium you wish, design a poster or bulletin board display entitled "American Folk Lore Figures." Accompany your display with a brief history of the figures you have illustrated.

CONGRATULATIONS, MINNESOTA

In 1858 the 32nd state, Minnesota, entered the Union.
(Same as #1 and #2 for Nevada, p. 63)

GLACIER PARK ESTABLISHED

Congress established Glacier National Park, Montana in 1910.
1. If you have ever visited this park and have pictures or photographs of your visit, prepare a display of them to share with others. Include a written explanation of each picture, or present your pictures with an oral explanation. Or, plan an imaginary trip.

TELEVISION PROGRAMS THREE TIMES A WEEK

In 1928 a Schenectady, New York station, WGY, began the first regularly scheduled television programs which were broadcast three times weekly.
1. Today television programs are broadcast daily in most areas. In some places they run 24 hours a day, 7 days a week. Pretend you are the program director of a local television station. Explain in writing the types of programs you think the station should broadcast and at what times of the day or night. Be sure to justify your choices.

12

HAPPY BIRTHDAY, MS. NIGHTINGALE

The famous English nurse, Florence Nightingale, was born in 1820.
1. Investigate and report on the life and contributions of this famous nurse.
2. If you are interested in a career related to nursing, investigate and report on that occupation. Include in your report the job's training and educational requirements, projected future

demand, benefits, advantages, disadvantages, salary, and other facts of interest.

EVENING WITH RADIO

According to *Radio Broadcast* magazine the number of people in 1922 who spent part of the evening listening to the radio was so large that it is incomprehensible.

1. How do you and other people spend your evenings today? Survey at least 25 people, both adults and children, to find out. Summarize and tabulate your results.

JAMESTOWN FOUNDED

In 1607 Jamestown was established.

1. Investigate the founding of this settlement and report on your findings.
2. Pretend you are a newspaper reporter who was sent by an English paper to report on the new settlement in Jamestown. Include in your news story background information about the founding of the town and describe how the residents live, what hardships they must endure, and why they feel it is worth it. Remember the five W's of news reporting.
3. Investigate and report on the quality of life which existed in the early settlements established in the colonies. What did people use for clothing, food, entertainment, shelter? How did they survive in the wilderness? What was a typical day like for a man and a woman?

AMERICA AT WAR WITH MEXICO
In 1846 Congress declared war on Mexico.

1. Investigate and report on the history of this war. Include in your report what was gained and lost by each side as a result.

FIRST U. S. OLYMPIC GAMES
St. Louis, Missouri was the site of the first U. S. Olympic Games held in 1904.

1. Investigate and report on the history of the Olympic Games. Include in your report the site of the next Olympic Summer and Winter Games.
2. Using any medium you wish, make a poster or bulletin board display showing the variety of events which are covered by the Winter and/or Summer Olympics.
3. Our Olympic team is supported by private donations. In some countries the government supports the teams. Create a poster using any medium you wish which will increase support of Americans for their Olympic teams by increasing donations to the Olympic fund.

STRAW HAT DAY

Well-dressed men consider this day to be the official date on which it is permissible to start wearing summer straw hats.
1. Make a collection of pictures or drawings illustrating changes in men's fashions. Be sure to indicate time periods associated with each picture.

REGULAR AIRMAIL SERVICE STARTED

The first regular airmail service was started by the U. S. Post Office in 1918. This first airmail route was between Washington, Philadelphia, and New York.
1. Pretend you have been assigned the task of designing a stamp commemorating this first airmail service. Use any medium you wish and make the denomination of the stamp the same as the price of a current first-class stamp.

CONGRESS RESTRICTS IMMIGRATION

In 1924 Congress passed a law restricting immigration to this country and making immigration follow a quota basis.
1. Investigate and report on the act which restricted immigration. Include in your report the name of this act and the patterns of immigration which led to the passage of the law.
2. Prepare a line, bar graph or chart showing patterns of immigration to this country.

FIRST AIRPLANE STEWARDESSES

United Airlines introduced a new service for its passengers—stewardesses—in 1930.

1. If the job of stewardess interests you, investigate and report on this occupation. Include in your paper a description of the duties, education and training requirements, salary, projected demand, benefits, advantages, and disadvantages.

GAS RATIONING STARTS

Rationing of gasoline started in 17 eastern states in 1942.

1. Although it has not been necessary to ration gas since the end of World War II, it may be necessary in the future as a means of conserving precious fuel. Think what it would mean to your family and their life style. What activities would you have to give up or curtail because of limited gas? How would your life change? Who in your family would be most affected? Write a report explaining these effects on you and your family.

16

FIRST "OSCAR" AWARDED

The Academy of Motion Picture Arts and Sciences awarded its first "Oscar" in 1929.

1. Assume you are a movie critic. Write a review of recent movies you have seen either on television or in the movie theaters. Pattern your critical review on one written by a professional. You may wish to read several samples in magazines or newspapers to see how a review is written.
2. Assume you are on the committee from the Academy of Motion Picture Arts and Sciences which has the task of recommending five movies released during the past year for "Best Picture of the Year." Write a report explaining why you think each of the five movies you list should be considered for this honor.
3. Investigate and report on "Oscars" which have been given out in the past for Best Picture of the Year. Present your data in chart form.

17

FIRST KENTUCKY DERBY

The first Kentucky Derby horse race was held in 1875.

1. If you have ever been to a horse race, illustrate your experience using any medium you wish.
2. Read a novel or story about horses and report on your reading using a format your teacher suggests.

FIRST SWITCHBOARD

The first telephone switchboard was installed in 1877; it served customers during the day and was a burglar alarm system at night.
1. Write a short story which includes these words: switchboard, burglar alarm, scared, nightly. Can you make your story have a surprise ending?

LAW REQUIRES SCHOOL ATTENDANCE

Massachusetts was the first state to pass a law in 1852 requiring children to attend school. At that time children between the ages of 8 and 14 were required to attend school for at least 12 weeks.
1. How do you feel about being required by state law to attend school for a specific number of days each year until you reach a certain age? Write a paper explaining your viewpoints on this subject. If you propose changes in the law, give your reasons.

COMET FRIGHTENS PEOPLE

In 1910 the famous Haley's Comet frightened thousands of people.
1. Investigate and report on the astrological phenomenon of comets. Indicate in your paper some of the famous comets of the past and any which are expected to appear in the future.
2. Use the appearance of a comet signifying the end of the world as a plot for a short story.

DANCING LESSONS COST 25 CENTS

An ad appearing in a Chicago newspaper in 1915 announced that modern dancing lessons cost 25 cents for 3½ hours.
1. If you enjoy dancing, demonstrate your talents for your classmates

FROG JUMPING JUBILEE

To commemorate Mark Twain's story, *The Celebrated Jumping Frog of Calaveras County,* Calaveras County, California holds an annual "Frog jumping jubilee." In 1928 the winner jumped 3 feet, 4 inches.

1. Use the idea of a frog-jumping contest as the main plot for a story.
2. Read the story by Mark Twain after which this event is named and report on your reading in a form your teacher suggests.

HOMESTEAD ACT

The Homestead Act became law in 1862.
1. Investigate and report on the significance and provisions of this act.

GIFT TO MADAME CURIE

In 1921 President Harding presented a capsule of radium to Madame Curie as a gift on behalf of the women of the U. S.
1. Investigate and report on the life and contributions of this woman scientist.

LINDBERGH CROSSES ATLANTIC

In 1927 Charles Lindbergh took off in his plane, "The Spirit of St. Louis," for Paris, attempting to win a prize for the first solo non-stop flight across the Atlantic.
1. Investigate and report on the life and contributions of this adventurous pilot.

FIRST WOMAN FLIES ACROSS ATLANTIC

In 1932 Amelia Earhart Putnam was the first woman to fly solo across the Atlantic.
1. Investigate and report on the life and contributions of this woman pilot.

21

BICYCLE A HAZARD

In 1819 New Yorkers got their first look at a vehicle called a bicycle which was ridden on the city streets. It was thought by many to be a hazard and so a law was passed which forbad its use in public places and on sidewalks.

1. Using any medium you wish, make a bulletin board or poster display of bicycle safety rules to follow.
2. Investigate the history of the bicycle. If possible, include in your report pictures or drawings of early models. Also include the outlook for future bicycle models and sales.

RED CROSS ORGANIZED

In 1881 the first Red Cross was organized in Washington by Clara Barton.

1. Investigate and report on the life and contributions of this woman.

"MYSTERY EXCURSION" TRAIN RIDE

To increase sales the Missouri Pacific Railroad began its "Mystery Excursion" ride between St. Louis and Arcadia, Missouri. People riding the train did not know, back in 1932, the city where they would end up until they arrived.

1. Use this sales promotion idea as a plot for a short story. Can you make your story have a surprise ending?

22

NATIONAL MARITIME DAY

This day commemorates the voyage of the Savannah, the first American-made steamship which sailed from Savannah, Georgia to Liverpool, England.

1. In honor of Maritime Day, prepare a bulletin board or poster display explaining boating or water safety rules.

BURR TRIED FOR TREASON

In 1807 Aaron Burr went on trial for treason.
  1. Investigate and report on the life and contributions of this statesman.

"GREAT TRAIN ROBBERY"

In 1868 the "great train robbery" took place when the Reno gang held up an Indianapolis-bound train at Marshfield, Indiana and stole $98,000 in cash.
  1. Use the title "The Great ___ Robbery" (you fill in the blank) as the plot for a short story.

 23

CAPTAIN KIDD HANGED

Captain William Kidd, charged with piracy and murder, was hanged in London in 1701.
  1. Read a novel or short story dealing with pirates and report on your reading in the format your teacher suggests.

BIFOCALS INVENTED

In 1785 Ben Franklin invented bifocal eyeglasses so he would not have to carry two pairs.
  1. Investigate and report on the life and contributions of this statesman/inventor.
  2. Explain in writing how wearing glasses helps correct vision and using drawings show how the use of glasses helps one to see both near and far. Also include suggestions to help eliminate eye strain.

 24

INDIANS SELL MANHATTAN FOR $24

Peter Minuit, founder of the New Amsterdam Colony, bought the island of Manhattan from the Indians for the equivalent of $24 in 1626.
  1. Investigate and report on the New Amsterdam Colony.

SECOND AMERICAN ENTERS SPACE

Malcolm Carpenter was the second American to go into orbit when he circled the earth 3 times in 1962.
1. Investigate and report on the life and contributions of this astronaut.

CONGRATULATIONS, SOUTH CAROLINA

South Carolina was the 8th state to enter the Union in 1788.
(Same as #1 and #2 for Nevada, p. 63)

MODEL "T" TO BE DISCONTINUED

In 1927 Henry Ford announced plans to discontinue manufacturing the Model "T" and replace it with the new model "A".
1. Write a report on the difference between the Model T and Model A.

"CRYPT OF CIVILIZATION"

In 1940 Oglethorpe University, Atlanta, Georgia placed thousands of objects representing daily life into a "Crypt of Civilization" which will not be opened until the year 8113.
1. Assume you were in charge of selecting objects representing life in the current year which would be placed in a crypt and not opened until the year 2050. Write a paper explaining what objects you would select and state your reasons for such selection.

TORNADOS DESTROY TOWN

In 1955 a series of tornados which killed 121 people lashed through several states in the middle west and completely destroyed the town of Udall, Kansas.
1. Investigate and report on the phenomenon of tornados. Include in your report an explanation of the causes of tornados and why they are so destructive. Also explain the "Tornado Belt."
2. Using any medium you wish, prepare a bulletin board or poster display showing the precautions you should take when a tornado strikes if you are either indoors or out.

MISSOURI COMPROMISE REPEALED

In 1854 the Kansas-Nebraska Act was passed which repealed the Missouri Compromise.
1. Investigate and report on the significance of this act and how it changed the provisions of the Missouri Compromise.

PRESIDENT JOHNSON SAVED BY A SINGLE VOTE

President Andrew Johnson who was on trial for impeachment charges was acquitted by a single vote in 1868.
1. Investigate and report on the impeachment process as stated in the Constitution.
2. Investigate and report on the background of President Andrew Jackson's impeachment trial.

FUNERAL SHIP DISCOVERED

In 1954 archeologists discovered the funeral ship of the Egyptian Pharaoh Cheops near the great pyramid of Giza in Egypt.
1. Investigate and report on the ancient Egyptian civilization and the customs associated with burying royalty.

HAPPY BIRTHDAY, MS. BLOOMER

This is the birthday of Amelia Bloomer who was born in 1818 and whose name was given to a form of women's dress called bloomers.
1. If you are fashion-minded try designing a fashion which might bear your name. Your design might be a drawing or an actual article you have made by sewing, knitting, crocheting, etc.
2. Bloomers were once fashionable but have since been replaced by other articles of apparel. Create a poster display of pictures and/or drawings showing fashion changes for women from the time of Ms. Bloomer's creation to the present time.

HAPPY BIRTHDAY, MS. HOWE

In 1819 Julia Ward Howe, a leader in the anti-slavery and women's vote movements, was born.

1. Investigate and report on the life and contributions of this woman.
2. Ms. Howe also wrote the lyrics for the "Battle Hymn of the Republic". Do you have talent at writing lyrics for a song? Try it. Pick any melody you like and try to compose a new set of lyrics. Submit your new lyrics and be sure to mention the name of the song to which they belong.

MONKEYS IN SPACE

Able and Baker, two monkeys, were confined in the nose of a rocket for a 300 mile trip into space in 1959.
1. Investigate and report on the history of America's space program. Include future projections for this program.
2. Use the theme of monkeys in space as a plot for a short story. Title your story, "Monkey Business."

CONGRATULATIONS, WISCONSIN

In 1848 the 30th state, Wisconsin, entered the Union.
(Same as #1 and #2 for Nevada, p. 63)

HAPPY BIRTHDAY, PRESIDENT KENNEDY

In 1917 the 35th president, John Kennedy, was born.
1. Investigate and report on the life and contributions of this president.

MT. EVEREST CONQUERED

Mt. Everest, the world's highest mountain, was conquered in 1953 when two climbers, Edmond Hillary and Tensing Norkay, reached the top.
1. Compose a short story about mountain climbers and the unusual things they see and find when they finally reach the top. Can you make this a surprise?

MEMORIAL DAY

This day is Memorial Day. Although it was originally set up as a legal holiday in many states to honor those who died in the Civil War, today it is observed to honor the memory of all war dead.

1. Some people consider Memorial Day "just another holiday" and seldom stop and think about the fighting men and women who gave their lives to ensure our country's democratic form of government and our personal liberties. Give some serious thought to the things you value which might have been lost had not thousands of men and women fought for them. Write an essay explaining your thoughts.
2. Using any medium you wish, design a coin, plate, or stamp which commemorates the celebration of Memorial Day and honors the war dead.
3. Using any medium you wish, design several different bumper stickers containing slogans appropriate to the celebration of Memorial Day.

"HALL OF FAME" DEDICATED

In 1901 the Hall of Fame was dedicated in New York City.

1. Prepare a report on one or more famous Americans who have been given a place of honor in the Hall of Fame.

HAPPY BIRTHDAY, MR. WHITMAN

The American poet and author, Walt Whitman, was born in 1819.

1. Using any medium you wish, illustrate one or more scenes from his works.
2. Investigate and report on the life and contributions of this writer.

RUSSIAN INVENTS TELEVISION

Moscow radio announced in 1951 that television was first invented by Boris Rosing, a Russian, back in 1907.

1. Investigate and report on the history of television. Include in your paper your forecast for the future of television.

May Game of the Month
Shopping Spree

No. of Players: 2, 3, or 4
Grade level: elementary
Materials: One large poster board with diagram (see page 218); one
small toy car for each player; one die; deck of 3 x 5 cards
containing shopping problems appropriate to ability of
age group playing game. Answers appear on reverse side.
Examples:

1 quart milk	.43
1 loaf bread	.53
	?
Plus 5% sales tax	?
You pay	?

4 loaves bread priced at 5 for $1.00   1 Television set
plus 2 quarts milk 3 for $1.00   priced $560
plus 4 heads lettuce, 3 for $1.00   Less 20% discount
          You pay __?__   You pay __?__

Rules:
1. Players decide by a convenient method who will go first. All
players' markers are in their respective garages. Each player must
travel around the board in the direction of the arrows during play.
2. The first player throws the die and advances his car the number of
spaces equal to the number shown on the die. If he lands on a
blank square, he draws a card and attempts to solve the problem.
When he has solved it, he turns over the card to check his answer.
If the answer is correct, he may stay where he is. If it is not, he
must return to his garage. If he lands on a penalty or bonus
square, he must follow those directions.
3. Play continues in this way with each player taking his turn at
drawing cards and solving problems. Should two players have a
collision by landing on the same square facing in opposite directions, both cars must return to their home garages and begin
again.
4. The winner is the first player who completes his shopping spree
around the town and returns to his garage.

Variation:
Include in card deck "free parking" cards which entitle players to remain in a penalty square without taking penalty.

DIRECTIONS FOR CONSTRUCTING SHOPPING SPREE GAME

The diagram for the Shopping Spree Game appears on this page. The number of squares may be increased or decreased to accommodate the size of posterboard used. Most of the squares on the gameboard should be left blank. Include a few penalty squares such, as Go back to Garage—flat tire, Go back to previous position, Miss a turn—Got Ticket for Speeding, etc. Also include a few bonus squares such as, Take another turn, Move ahead 3 spaces, etc.

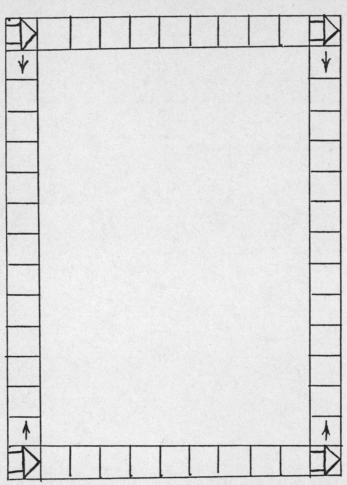

Chapter Ten

June

1

HAPPY BIRTHDAY, MR. MARQUETTE

The explorer Jacques Marquette was born in 1637.
   1. Investigate and report on the life and contributions of this explorer.

CONGRATULATIONS, KENTUCKY

The 15th state, Kentucky, was admitted to the Union in 1792.
   (Same as #1 and #2 for Nevada, p. 63)

CONGRATULATIONS, TENNESSEE

Tennessee, the 16th state, was admitted to the Union in 1792.
   (Same as #1 and #2 for Nevada, p. 63)

2

FIRST NIGHT BASEBALL GAME

The first baseball game played at night took place in Ft. Wayne, Indiana in 1883.
   1. Investigate and report on the history of baseball.

INDIANS BECOME CITIZENS

Congress made all American Indians citizens of the U. S. in 1924.
   1. Investigate and report on the topic, "Government Treatment of the American Indian." At the end of your paper state your

conclusion about whether treatment of Indians by the government has been fair and give reasons for your opinion.
2. If you know anyone who is of American Indian descent, interview him to get his viewpoint on the topic, "Government Treatment of the American Indian." Write a paper summarizing the results of your interview.
3. Investigate and report on one or more Indian tribes which live in your area or in which you have a personal or historical interest. Include in your report a description of how the tribe lives, the kinds of food they eat, their religion, and their cultural heritage.
4. Make a display of articles, pictures and/or Indian artifacts or handicrafts, or make a collection of Indian food recipes including as many illustrations as possible.
5. If you like to cook, make one or two Indian dishes to share with your classmates. Prepare a copy of each recipe giving exact measurements and directions. Compute the cost of each serving.

3

"CASEY AT THE BAT"

In 1888 the poem, "Casey at the Bat" written by Ernest L. Thayer was published for the first time.
1. Read this famous baseball poem. Using any medium you wish, illustrate a scene from it.
2. If you are a baseball fan, compose your own version of _____ At the Bat, inserting a name which you feel is appropriate.

MT. PALOMAR GETS TELESCOPE

On this day in 1948 the dedication of the world's largest telescope at Mt. Palomar Observatory, California took place.
1. Investigate and report on the topic of telescopes. Include in your report an explanation of how a telescope works and the locations of some of the largest telescopes.

FIRST HUMAN SATELLITE

In 1965 two astronauts, James McDivitt and Edward White, began their four-day orbital flight in Gemini Four. White became the first human satellite when he floated in space supported by a line carrying oxygen.

    1. Investigate and report on the life and contributions of one or both of these astronauts.

ROQUEFORT CHEESE INVENTED

On this day in 1070 the first Roquefort cheese was accidentally invented by a monk. He returned to the lunch he had left uneaten several days ago and found the sheep's milk cheese had developed a new flavor. He liked it so much that he hurried down to the local monastery near Roquefort, France to share it with the other monks.

    1. Investigate and report on the manufacture of different types of cheeses.

    2. Make a recipe collection of your family's favorite cheese dishes. Write each on a separate paper using your best handwriting. Be sure to give complete instructions and exact measurements. If desired, illustrate some of the recipes using any medium you wish. Be sure to include yield of each recipe and cost per serving.

FORD GETS TRIAL RUN

Henry Ford drove his first car around the streets of Detroit for a trial run in 1896.

    1. Investigate and report on the life and contributions of this automobile manufacturer.

BANANAS INTRODUCED

Visitors to the Centennial Exposition in Philadelphia in 1876 were introduced to the first bananas which sold for 10 cents a piece.

    1. Investigate and report on how and where this fruit is raised, conditions which affect its growth, and its uses.

    2. Prepare a map of the world, either free-hand drawn or traced, showing areas of the world in which bananas are raised.

    3. Make a collection of your family's favorite banana recipes.

4. Assume you are in charge of advertising for the banana growers association. Using any medium you wish, create an advertisement that will encourage people to use more bananas.

"MARSHALL PLAN" INVENTED

In 1947 Secretary of State, George Marshall, described his plan for the economic recovery of Europe.
1. Investigate and report on the Marshall Plan. Explain its major points and its significance.

YEAR OF NO SUMMER

Strange as it may sound, in 1816 the weather was unusually cold and ten inches of snow fell in New England, beginning what was known as the "year in which there was no summer."
1. Investigate weather bureau statistics to determine how unusual snowfall is during the spring and summer months in your region. Prepare a line or bar graph or chart illustrating the statistics you collect.

EGGS 17 CENTS DOZEN

Philadelphia newspapers in 1904 launched a campaign directed toward dropping the cost of living. The papers listed the following examples of the high cost of living: eggs 17 cents a dozen, cream 10 cents a pint, chickens 40 cents a piece, half a ham, 70 cents.
1. Collect statistics which compare the cost of living today with the cost of living in 1904. Compare the prices of the items mentioned in local stores and compile a chart or graph illustrating the statistics you collect.

FIRST DRIVE-IN THEATER

The first motion-picture drive-in opened in Camden, New Jersey in 1933.
1. Using any medium you wish, create an advertisement appropriate to a new motion picture which has recently been released which you think everyone should see.

D-DAY

In 1944 the Allies launched their D-Day invasion on the beaches of Normandy.
1. Investigate and report on the D-Day invasion. Include in your report the major events leading up to this invasion and the invasion's significance to the end of the war.
2. Prepare a time line using any medium you wish showing major events leading up to and including World War II.

BOONE STARTS EXPLORATION

Daniel Boone started to explore Kentucky in 1769.
1. Investigate and report on the life and contributions of this frontiersman.
2. Compose a short story in which you and Daniel Boone are the principal characters.

FIRST DIME NOVEL

In 1860 the first "dime novel" was published.
1. The "dime" or inexpensive novel is available today and called the paperback. Read a paperback novel and report on your reading using the format your teacher suggests.
2. Compile a list of paperback novels which you feel are interesting and appropriate to people your age. Divide your list into categories such as books boys will like or girls will like, mysteries, non-fiction, fiction, etc. Be sure to include the complete title, author, publisher, where the book is available, and a brief summary of the story or contents.

ICE CREAM MANUFACTURED

In 1786 Mr. Hull advertised in a New York newspaper that he would start producing ice cream commercially.
1. Investigate and report on the production of commercial ice cream. If possible, visit an ice cream manufacturing plant in your area and describe your visit as part of your report.

VACUUM CLEANER PATENTED

In 1869 Ives W. McGaffey received a patent for the invention of the vacuum cleaner.

1. Investigate and report on the topic of patents.
2. Write a paper entitled, "My Life as a Vacuum Cleaner."

"MARK TWAIN" ORIGIN EXPLAINED

Samuel Clemens explained the origins of his pen name, Mark Twain, in 1877.

1. Try to find out the origins of Samuel Clemens' pen name.

WILSON DEMANDS FREEDOM OF SEAS

President Wilson sent a note to Germany demanding freedom of the seas after the Lusitania was sunk in 1915.

1. Prepare a time line of major events leading up to and including World War I.

COMMITTEE DRAFTS DECLARATION OF INDEPENDENCE

In 1776 a committee made up of Thomas Jefferson, John Adams, Benjamin Franklin, Roger Sherman, and Robert R. Livingston was appointed to draft the Declaration of Independence.

1. Investigate and report on the life and contributions of one or more of these committee members.
2. Read the Declaration of Independence and state its major points in your own words.

MARINES INVADE CUBA

The invasion of Cuba during the Spanish-American War was begun by the U. S. Marines in 1898.

1. Investigate and report on this war. Include in your paper an explanation of events which led to the war between these two countries and what was gained and lost as a result.

11

HAPPY BIRTHDAY, KING KAMEHAMEHA 1

On this day the Hawaiian leader, King Kamehameha I, was born.
1. Investigate and report on the life and contributions of this leader.
2. Using any medium you wish, create a map, free-hand drawn or traced, of Hawaii. Show on your map the state's major cities, principal city, and major industries.

SILVER DISCOVERED

In 1859 the Comstock Silver Lode was discovered. This proved to be one of the greatest silver discoveries of all time.
1. Write a report on the topic of silver. Include in your report how and where it is mined and uses for this ore.

12

VIRGINIA BILL OF RIGHTS

In 1776 the Virginia Bill of Rights was written by George Mason.
1. Try your hand at writing a students' or teachers' bill of rights. Use your best handwriting and if desired, illustrate one or more of the points. Your bill of rights should have at least 10 items.

BASEBALL INVENTED

In 1839 a game whose rules required a diamond-shape field and 9 players was created by Abner Doubleday.
1. Investigate and report on the history of baseball. Include in your paper some of the changes in the rules of play from the time of its invention.
2. Construct a line or bar graph, or chart for one or more of the following: major league teams' won/lost record; All-star participation of major league teams; batting average for each team in the major leagues; number of runs earned by each team in the major leagues in a particular year; or other information of interest to you.

HOUDINI PERFORMS MAJOR FEAT

In 1923 Harry Houdini, the famous magician, freed himself from a straight jacket while hanging 40 feet from the ground in a head-down position.

1. Investigate and report on the life and contributions of this famous magician.
2. If you enjoy performing magic tricks, give a short presentation to your classmates.

PRESIDENT'S WIFE SERVES ICE CREAM

To the delight of all her guests, Mrs. Washington served ice cream during a dinner party in 1789.

1. Investigate and report on types of foods eaten during the early days of the our country's history. Find out if any of the foods or dishes created then have survived the test of time and are still prepared and popular today.

SENATOR LONG TALKS LONG TIME

Senator Huey Long spoke for 15 hours, 35 minutes during his filibuster against the National Recovery Administration in 1935.

1. Investigate and report on the origins and use of the filibuster.

TODAY IS FLAG DAY

1. Prepare a bulletin board or poster display of rules to observe in displaying the American flag.

STARS AND STRIPES OFFICIAL

In 1777 the Continental Congress made the stars and stripes the official flag.

1. Investigate and report on the history of our flag. If possible, include with your report illustrations of some of the early flags.

WASHINGTON TAKES CHARGE OF ARMY

George Washington was appointed Commander-in-Chief of the Continental Army in 1775.

    1. Investigate and report on the life and contributions of this general/president.

CONGRATULATIONS, ARKANSAS

The 25th state, Arkansas, was admitted into the Union in 1836. (Same as #1 and #2 for Nevada, p. 63)

FATHERS DAY

It may not always fall on the 16th of June. The third Sunday in June is known as Father's Day.

    1. Write a paper entitled "The Man I Admire the Most."

WORLD COURT ORGANIZED

The World Court, which was part of the League of Nations, was organized on this day.

    1. Investigate and report on the functions and organization of this court.

FIRST WOMAN IN SPACE

In 1963, Valentina Tereshkova, the first woman space traveler, was launched into orbit from Russia.

    1. Write a paper entitled, "Famous Women Scientists."
    2. Would you like to travel in space? If your answer is yes, write a paper explaining the training you would go through as an astronaut.

BATTLE OF BUNKER HILL

The famous Battle of Bunker Hill took place in 1775 when 3,500 British soldiers attacked 1,000 American patriots. Because of a lack of ammunition the Americans were told, "Don't shoot until you see the whites of their eyes!"

1. Pretend you are a newspaper reporter assigned to cover this story. Write a newspaper account of this famous battle. Remember the five W's of news reporting.
2. Using any medium you wish, prepare an illustration of this famous battle. You may wish to refer to a history book so that you can draw the clothes accurately.
3. The Battle of Bunker Hill was the beginning of the Revolutionary War. Create a time line listing major events leading up to and including the Revolutionary War.

FIRST WOMAN PASSENGER FLIES ACROSS ATLANTIC

In 1928 Amelia Earhart was the first woman passenger to fly across the Atlantic Ocean.

1. Create a short story entitled, The First Woman to _____. (you decide what).

CONGRESS DECLARES WAR ON ENGLAND

In 1812 Congress declared war on Great Britian, for the second time.

1. Create a time line showing major events leading up to and including the War of 1812.
2. How do you feel about war? Write a serious essay explaining your views and giving reasons for your way of thinking.

HAPPY BIRTHDAY, MR. GEHRIG

The famous baseball player, Lou Gehrig, was born in 1903.

1. Investigate and report on the life and contributions of this famous baseball star.
2. Make a baseball collage or mobile containing various symbols of the game. If making a mobile, use a coat hanger as your base.

F. C. C. CREATED

In 1934 the Federal Communications Commission was created by Congress.

1. Investigate and report on the functions, organization, and purpose of this commission.
2. If you had the responsibility and authority to regulate television shows, what types of programs would you prevent television stations from broadcasting? Write a paper explaining your thoughts on this subject and giving reasons for your position.

OFFICIAL SEAL ADOPTED

In 1782 Congress adopted an official seal of the U. S. using a design made by William Barton.

1. Using any medium you wish, create one or more designs appropriate for the official seal of the U. S.

CONGRATULATIONS, WEST VIRGINIA

The 25th state, West Virginia, was admitted into the Union in 1863. (Same as #1 and #2 for Nevada, p. 63)

LONG-PLAYING RECORDS DEMONSTRATED

In 1948 the first long-playing record was demonstrated by Dr. Peter Goldmark.

1. Investigate and report on the manufacture of records and how and where recordings are made.
2. Pretend you have been assigned the task of designing the jacket for the first long-playing record. Using any medium you wish and any title you wish for the record, create an attractive jacket.
3. Conduct a survey among your friends or relatives to determine their favorite long-playing record albums. Summarize

the results of your survey in chart form. Draw conclusions based on your survey about the types of music people of different age groups enjoy.

SMOKER'S DEATH RATE
97.5% HIGHER THAN NONSMOKERS

In 1954 the American Cancer Society reported that heavy smokers from 50 to 70 years of age have a death rate that is 97.5% higher than those who do not smoke.

1. Make a bar or line graph showing smoker versus non-smoker statistics. Consult your local cancer, heart, or lung association for figures for your report.
2. Make a poster showing reasons why one should not smoke.

DEPARTMENT OF JUSTICE ESTABLISHED

In 1870 Congress established the U. S. Department of Justice.

1. Investigate and report on the organization and functions of this department of government.
2. Write an essay on the meaning of justice from the viewpoint of a student.

SCIENCE OF OSTEOPATHY FOUNDED

Dr. Andrew Taylor started the science of osteopathy in 1874.

1. If you have an interest in a medically-related career, investigate and report on the occupation of your choice. Include in your paper the education and training requirements, projected future demand, benefits, advantages, disadvantages, beginning salary, and why you feel this is the career for you.
2. Make a diagram (free-hand or traced) of the human skeletal system and identify the major parts.

PENN'S PEACE TREATY

In 1883 William Penn signed a peace treaty with the Leni-Lenape Indians.

1. Using any medium you wish, prepare an illustration of this historical moment.

TYPEWRITER PATENTED

Christopher Sholes received a patent in 1868 for a machine called the typewriter which only typed capital letters.
1. If you have access to a typewriter at school or home, do some artistic typing by creating a design using one or more letters in repetition.

CIVIL AERONAUTICS AUTHORITY ORGANIZED

The Civil Aeronautics Authority was created by Congress in 1938.
1. Investigate and report on the organization and functions of this government agency.

FLYING SAUCERS REPORTED

Kenneth Arnold of Boise, Idaho reported the first flying saucer in 1947.
1. Investigate and report on the topic, "Flying Saucers—Real or Imagined?" At the conclusion of your report reach your own decision but try to present both viewpoints.
2. Use the sighting of flying saucers as the main plot for a short story.
3. Using your imagination or information from reported sightings of flying saucers and in whatever medium you wish, illustrate some flying saucers.
4. Investigate and report on the topic, "Does Life Exist on Other Planets?". Be sure to document your report and at the conclusion reach your own decision on the question.

SMOKING INJURIOUS TO HEALTH

In 1964 the U.S. Federal Trade Commission announced that cigarette manufacturers would be required to place a warning about smoking being dangerous to health on all cigarette packages.
1. Using any medium you wish, prepare a poster or bulletin board display entitled, "Warning: Smoking May Be Dangerous to Your Health "

TABLE FORKS INTRODUCED

In 1630 Governor John Winthrop brought the table fork with him to the New World and introduced it to America.

1. Many beautiful designs, some intricate and some simple, are placed on forks and other silverware. Using a black and white medium of your choice, create several designs which would be suitable for engraving on silverware.
2. Make a fork sculpture of discarded plastic, wood, or metal forks and/or other silverware. You may glue the pieces together or tie them together with string or colorful yarn. Be sure to give your sculpture a name.

CUSTER'S LAST STAND

In 1876 General George Custer and his force of 208 men were killed at the Battle of the Little Big Horn.

1. Prepare a shoebox diorama of this famous battle.
2. Pretend you are a reporter for a weekly news magazine who has been sent to cover this story. Remember the five W's of news reporting. Be sure to give your readers a background of events leading up to this story.

YELLOW FEVER FIGHT

In 1900 Dr. Walter Reed began a campaign to eliminate the disease, yellow fever.

1. Investigate and report on the life and contributions of this famous doctor.
2. If you are interested in a medically-related career, investigate and report on the occupation in which you are interested. Include in your report the training and educational requirements, projected demand, expected beginning salary, advan-

tages and disadvantages, fringe benefits, and why you feel this would be the right career for you.

HAPPY BIRTHDAY, MS. KELLER

In 1880 Helen Keller, an author, was born both blind and deaf.
1. Investigate and report on the life and contributions of this famous woman.
2. Investigate and report on the invention of Braille which allows blind people to read.
3. Investigate and report on the invention of sign language which allows deaf people to talk.

AMERICA BUYS CANAL

In 1902 the U. S. bought the uncompleted Panama Canal from France.
1. Investigate and report on the history of the Panama Canal.

VENDING MACHINES FOR EGGS

In 1938 machines dispensing hard-boiled eggs were installed throughout the state of Pennsylvania as a way of helping farmers dispose of an egg surplus.
1. Prepare a recipe collection of egg dishes. Be sure to copy each in your best handwriting giving exact directions, ingredients, and yield per recipe. If you wish, illustrate a few of the recipes using any medium you wish. Indicate the cost per serving of each recipe and its source.

WORLD WAR I STARTS AND ENDS

An incident which started World War I occurred on this day in 1914, and the treaty ending World War I was signed on this same day in 1919.
1. Investigate and compare these two events.

29

HAPPY BIRTHDAY, DR. MAYO

In 1861 the founder of the Mayo Clinic, William James Mayo, was born.
1. Investigate and report on the life and contributions of this famous doctor.

30

TEAPOT DOME SCANDALS

The three people involved in the "Teapot Dome Scandals" were indicted in 1924.
1. Investigate and report on this famous government scandal. Contrast this scandal with the recent Watergate scandal. How were they similar? How were they different?

GONE WITH THE WIND PUBLISHED

The novel, *Gone with the Wind*, a story about the Civil War, was published in 1936.
1. Prepare a time line showing major events leading up to and including the Civil War.
2. Using any medium you wish, illustrate one or more scenes from this famous Civil War story.

June Game of the Month
Math Wheel

No. of Players: 2, 3, or 4
Grade level: elementary
Materials: One Math Wheel Diagram on posterboard (See page 237 for diagram); 4 markers of different colors (use poker chips, bottle caps, buttons, wooden cubes, etc.) and 1 die.

Rules:
1. Players decide by a convenient method who will go first.
2. The teacher or players will decide what basic arithmetic operation they will use for the game: addition, multiplication, or division.

Each player places his marker in one of the "X" marked segments on the outer-circle of the board.

3. The first player throws the die and advances the number of segments on the outer-most concentric circle going in a clock-wise direction as indicated on the die. This new position can be maintained by the player if he can perform the arithmetic operation agreed upon with all of the numbers involved in the concentric circles equal to the number shown on the die. For example, using the diagram, assume the operation to be addition and the player began with his marker on the outer-most concentric circle in the segment marked X, the segment containing the No. 4. He threw the die and obtained the number 3. He would then move his marker into the outer-most segment numbered 5, advancing three spaces. The player would then be required to add 5 plus 8 plus 3 and get the correct answer of 16. The player may do the addition in his head or on paper. If the player gets the correct answer the first try, he may remain on his new position and the next player takes his turn. If the player does not achieve a correct answer on the first try, he must return his marker to the position where he was before throwing the die.

4. If the basic operation agreed upon was multiplication, using the same situations described above, the player would be expected to multiply the numbers represented in the outermost three concentric circles on the wheel. Example $5 \times 8 = 40 \times 3 = 120$.

5. If the basic operation agreed upon is division, using the situation described above, the player would be expected to use the numbers represented in the outer-most three concentric circles as the dividend, 583, and divide by the number shown in the inner-most concentric circle in that segment of the wheel, 2. Therefore, the problem to be solved would be $583 \div 2 = 291$, remainder 1, or if decimals have been studied, the answer would be 291.5

6. Only one marker may be in any segment at one time. Therefore, should a player move into a segment already occupied by another player, the second player must go back to the position occupied before throwing the die.

7. The first player to move completely around the board and reach his starting position is the winner.

Variations:

1. For a longer game, require more revolutions around the board.
2. If negative numbers have been studied, the arithmetic operation of subtraction may be used. Following the example used above, the player would subtract $5 - 8 = (-3) - (3) = 0$.

3. For more advanced classes, two or three digit numbers may be placed inside each segment of the concentric circles.
4. If decimals have been studied, the teacher may add numbers which contain decimals.
5. If fractions have been studied, the teacher may place fractions inside the segments.

DIRECTIONS FOR CONSTRUCTING MATH WHEEL GAME

Redraw the diagram shown on page 237 on a large posterboard. In the innermost concentric circle, write in each segment in random order the numbers 0 through 9. In the remaining segments of the remaining six concentric circles write in random order the numbers 0 through 9. See blow-up on page 237. To indicate starting positions, mark an "X" in one of the outermost segments in the outermost concentric circle. Place another "X" in another segment within the same concentric circle 30 spaces away. Continue this until there are four "X's" placed 30 segments apart.

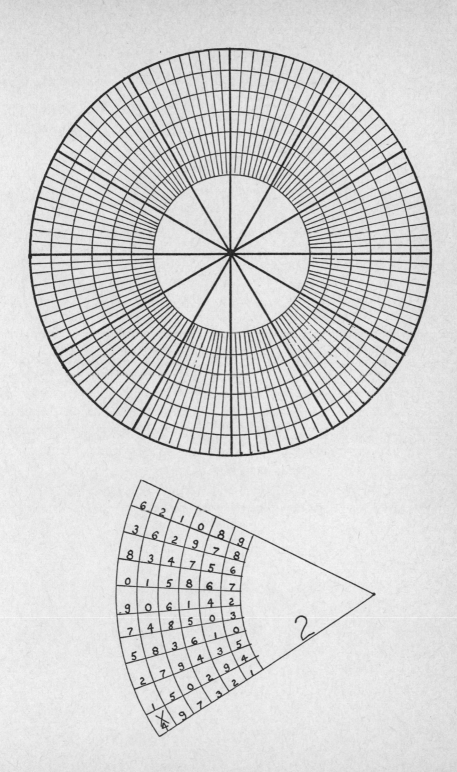

BIBLIOGRAPHY

_____. *Chase Calendar of Events.* Flint, Michigan: Apple Tree Press, 1975

Douglas, George William, *The American Book of Days.* New York: H.W. Wilson Company, 1937

Mirkin, Stanford M., *When Did It Happen.* New York: Ives Washburn, Inc., (a division of David McKay Co., Inc.), 1957

INDEX